THE MISSION-CENTERED LIFE

Following Jesus into the Broken Places

Bethany Ferguson

STUDY GUIDE

New
Growth
Press

WWW.NEWGROWTHPRESS.COM

New Growth Press, Greensboro, NC 27404
www.newgrowthpress.com

Cover Design: Faceout Books, faceoutstudio.com
Interior Typesetting and eBook: lparnellbookservices.com

ISBN 978-1-948130-67-7 (Print)
ISBN 978-1-948130-68-4 (ebook)

Printed in the United States of America

26 25 24 23 22 21 20 19   2 3 4 5 6

Contents

Introduction

> Now to him who is able to do immeasurably
> more than all we ask or imagine, according to his
> power that is at work within us, to him be glory
> in the church and in Christ Jesus throughout all
> generations, for ever and ever! Amen.
> —Ephesians 3:20–21 (NIV)

Three a.m., no moon, and I'm shuffling up the second tallest mountain in Africa. In the last forty-eight hours, I've been robbed and rained on, and I had a stressful interaction with an alcoholic park guide. I'm dirty, freezing, and feeling the impact of insufficient caffeine consumption. The journey isn't even halfway over yet, and I'm longing for comfort and home.

As my feet fight for traction on the Mount Kenya trail, I watch gravel and loose rock roll back down the mountain, and I pray that I won't fall with those scattering stones. I wonder (not for the first time), *How in the world did I get here?*

It's important for you to know that I am not the most athletic or the most adventurous. One of my earliest childhood memories is of being out on the soccer field, paying attention to the weeds at my feet, completely oblivious to the action around me. I am not the person you would pick to scale mountains, raft rivers, or respond to drunk park guides for whom English is a second language. I am a fan of lattes and pedicures and reliable internet.

I love home and settledness, family and tradition, patterns and rhythms, and things you can count on. But as much as I love home, I'm enamored by the beauty and diversity of our world, and I'm broken-hearted over the injustice and disparity that seem universal.

This love of the world has led me to leave home multiple times. Opportunity, interest, and what I believe to be calling converged, allowing me to spend most of the last fifteen years in East Africa, particularly Uganda, South Sudan, and now Kenya.

In each of those places, I started out a stranger and ended up making a home. I found new patterns and rhythms and things to count on. But I've also been confronted with the fact that our world is more broken than I initially thought, that I myself am fearful, and that I'm not as nice or competent as I used to think. In fact, I'm just as likely to mess things up as to be helpful. To climb a mountain seems hard, but to transform places of poverty and trauma and loss—well, that's pretty much impossible.

But I believe in a God who does impossible things. One who brings water from rocks, makes dead things alive, and is making everything new. A God who always is doing more than we can ask or imagine. A God of resurrection.

This God also loves the poor and the unjustly accused, the fearful and the lonely, the depressed and the angry, the sinner and the stranger, and the saint. He understands our longing for home and has promised to prepare a place for us. For those of us reborn in him, we have a calling to bring God's love into places of poverty, injustice, and isolation. We can begin to bring tastes of home to the wilderness.

Now, I'm not saying you need to move to Uganda or South Sudan (though maybe you should consider doing that). And I'm not saying you have to become a missionary or give away your possessions or start preaching all the time (though I'm not ruling those things out).

What I am saying is this: God's grace reorders our lives so that we move out from ourselves and toward those who need to receive what seems as yet impossible. Paradoxically, as we move out from ourselves, we also gain more for ourselves because God meets us in new ways with the good news of his love for us.

I have a friend who jokingly said, "I was so nervous to become a Christian and to ask for God's calling on my life because I just knew God would call me to leave everything and move to the middle of Africa." I cannot disprove that concern because when God began working in my life, I did leave everything and move to the middle of Africa. I still look around and wonder how I got here. But I also know that finding life in the broken places has been a great gift of God to me.

The gift God has for you will not look the same as mine. But grace and love and mission are woven into all our days, so it is important to pay attention to how God's Spirit is calling you and bringing them into your story.

I would be lying if I said I didn't want you to be a little bit impressed by the image of me scaling a challenging mountain. And part of me also wants you to see that working in areas of injustice and poverty is an exciting adventure, full of accomplishment and mountaintop experiences.

But in more than a decade of international work, I've learned that this life is also marked by seasons of valleys, seasons of deserts, seasons of doubt, and sometimes seasons of death. And it is often in these unglamorous, unexciting, and grief-filled places that God shows us new parts of his redemptive work.

A year after the Mount Kenya climb, I found myself in a valley of sorts. Much of the work I did in South Sudan seemed to be crumbling: cities I had worked in had destabilized, and people I cared about had fled from their homes. Some of them had died.

I returned from Kenya for a season in the United States. There I reconnected with friends who, while I was fumbling through life in East Africa, had built beautiful homes and families. In what felt to me like a sharp contrast, I was able to fit all my earthly belongings into two footlockers.

I was frustrated by the complexities of working in areas of poverty and injustice, and I wondered if it was all worth it. I looked at the racial sins and injustices in my passport country and read articles about how people trying to help in Africa were actually hurting things, and I wondered how we kept getting it so wrong. I wondered if I had chased the mountaintop experiences but missed the reality that things weren't actually getting better.

I was longing for home, but I had no idea how to find it.

God gave me grace in that valley of homesickness by allowing me to write this book. It is a reminder of the grace that followed me up the mountain and also met me in the valley. This grace is wider and more beautiful than I imagined. It meets me—meets us—in the confidence and in the questions, in the adventure and in the mundane, in our living rooms and at the ends of the earth, on the mountaintops and in the valleys.

Maybe you are wondering how God's grace redirects your life, and you are looking for what it means to live missionally right where you are. Perhaps you are considering stepping into areas of poverty or injustice, whether in a place across town or across the globe. Maybe you have been working in these areas for a while and are wondering how you got here or what will sustain you. Maybe you're wondering if it is all worth it.

As I have reflected on these same questions, a pattern has emerged: as we experience God's grace in our lives, it frees us to move out into the world. But that movement into a needy world brings new struggles.

It causes us to grow still closer to God and receive more of his love in fresh ways. This in turn moves us out still farther into places that are desperate to know the grace we've received, and the pattern repeats.

This book is about rhythms of missional living. It is about how God meets us, moves us forward, gives us reasons to celebrate, and draws us deeper into himself. It is about finding possibilities within the impossible and being transformed as we discover grace in the broken places.

Three a.m., climbing Mount Kenya, wondering how I got there, I happened to look up.

Like never before, I experienced my own neediness and the world's unfairness on this journey up the mountain. But for some reason, in that moment, I was overcome with joy. Perhaps my thinking was clouded due to less oxygen at such an altitude. But I believe the joy came then because we often experience God's richest grace in the midst of the hardest struggles.

As I looked up, I saw my small band of friends who agreed to join me in this craziness even though none of us had any idea what we were actually signing up for. I knew that together we were fighting for breath, rest, encouragement, and laughter. Looking higher, I couldn't see the top of mountain because it was still so dark. But because I saw a glimpse of it through the clouds the day before, I knew that somewhere high above was the end of this particular climb, and rumor had it we'd see the miracle of equatorial snow. Tilting my head farther, I saw the brilliance of constellations and planets, so close I felt I could almost touch them. In the midst of night's deepest darkness, my path was paved with unexpected brightness seen only because the lights I usually depended on were absent. With friends, surrounded by stars and anticipating the dawn, I reached for a deep breath and gratefully took the next step in the darkness, knowing that I was finding my way home.

How to Use
This Study

The Mission-Centered Life is organized into ten lessons designed for people who want to explore their role in building Christ's kingdom. Like the other small group resources in the *Gospel-Centered Life* series, this study has a gospel focus. That means you will not merely study missions but will do so in a way that keeps your eyes on Jesus and the good news of his love and power to save. You will consider how this gospel propels you to go out and love your neighbors, including people who might be far away or very different from you.

The Mission-Centered Life will help you consider this in a group study. Studying with others lets you benefit from what God is also teaching them, and it gives you encouragement as you apply what you learn.

The group will be a place to share not only successes but also sins and worries and weaknesses, so expect differences in how people participate. It's okay if some in the group are cheery while others are weary, or if some are eager to share while others take it slowly. But because you'll be studying the Bible and praying together, also expect God's Spirit to work and change people—starting with you!

Each participant should have one of these study guides in order to join in reading and follow the discussion questions. Several questions require looking at lists or charts in the study guide.

The leader should read through each lesson before it begins, but participants do not need to complete any preparation or homework. Each lesson includes optional material for further study on your own, but you will be able to participate fully in each group session even if you don't do the on-your-own studies.

The Mission-Centered Life is a topical study. Each lesson examines a key aspect of missional life. You might notice that this study also loosely follows the gospel of John, returning often to that book in the Bible to draw on the story of Jesus's own mission to the world.

Each lesson will take about an hour to complete, and includes these elements:

BIG IDEA. This is a summary of the main teaching of the lesson.

BIBLE CONVERSATION. You will read a passage or passages from the Bible and discuss what you have read. As the heading suggests, the Bible conversation questions are intended to spark a conversation rather than generate correct answers. In most cases, the questions will have several possible good answers. Answers are not provided in the book, but are left for your group to discover as you examine the Bible text and consider how it applies.

ARTICLE. This is the main teaching section of the lesson, written by the book's author. It includes observations from her own life on mission. Some names have been changed in the articles and essays to protect the privacy of others.

DISCUSSION. The discussion questions following the article will help you apply the teaching to your life. Again, there will be several good ways to answer each question.

PRAYER. Prayer is a critical part of the lesson because your spiritual growth will happen through God's work in you, not by your self-effort. You will be asking him to do that good work. If your group is large, it may help to split up to pray so that everyone has a better chance to participate.

ESSAY. The essay contains further teaching and reflections from the book's author for you to read on your own if you want to do further study. Additional Bible readings are also included in some lessons.

REFLECTION. Questions for reflection follow each essay. Most people find it helpful to write down their responses, perhaps in a journal. Journaling can help you clarify your thoughts and remember them, and it can serve as a starting point for personal prayer.

The mission-centered life is about Jesus, who proclaimed, "I came that they may have life" (John 10:10). In this study, you will see his love for the world he made and all its people. And you will hear his call for you as well to come nearer to him and to join in his life-giving mission.

1

Going

BIG IDEA

Mission begins when we encounter a God who rescues us from our own brokenness and invites us to be instruments of healing in a broken world.

Everywhere we look, we are confronted by the paradox of a world that is both beautiful and broken. We are people made in the image of God, but we are also people who have disobeyed God and struggle daily to live as he designed. Before you can begin thinking about living a mission-centered life, you must first see that the goal of mission is the redemption and renewal of all things, in Christ. And that change starts with broken, sinful people who encounter Jesus and are redeemed and made new. In other words, it starts with you.

BIBLE CONVERSATION

The Bible tells us that when God first created all things, including us, "God saw everything that he had made, and behold, it was very good" (Genesis 1:31). But not everything is very good anymore, so let's consider what we've become and where we are headed. Read the passages and discuss the questions below.

1. Read **Genesis 3:1–6**. The outward sin of eating some fruit might not seem so bad, but what deeper attitudes toward their Creator are behind the man and woman's disobedience? List several attitudes, especially any you can relate to.

2. Continue by reading **Genesis 3:7–13**. In what ways are the woman and man no longer very good but are now broken? How can you tell that they've become entrenched in sin and selfishness?

3. Go further by reading **Genesis 3:14–19**. List some sufferings and hostilities in the world today that are part of these curses. Which of them have you experienced most deeply?

At the end of the Bible, Revelation 21:4 gives a vision of a new heaven and a new earth where God lives with his people and "he will wipe away every tear from their eyes, and death shall be no more, neither shall there be mourning, nor crying, nor pain anymore, for the former things have passed away."

4. Now read **Revelation 22:1–5**. What do you find most appealing about this vision of the future earth and the people who live there? Explain why you like it.

5. How does this ending to Christ's work motivate you to join in his mission to spread his kingdom throughout the world? Think of several ways.

✶✶✶✶

Now read the following article together and discuss the questions at the end. Read the article aloud, taking turns at the paragraph breaks.

Lesson

ARTICLE

Beauty and Brokenness

The Bible opens with this familiar cadence: "In the beginning, God created the heavens and the earth" (Genesis 1:1). Genesis goes on to describe, in more specificity, the creation of the world we inhabit and the goodness of this world. Haven't you experienced this goodness? In the lingering glow of a summer sunset as you sip iced tea and watch fireflies. In the crisp fall air, as leaves change and scarves become the perfect thing. In the quiet of a clean layer of freshly fallen snow. In the hopeful unfurling of new life with the greenness of spring. Every season offers the magical rhythms of a glorious world that, in spite of itself, points to the goodness of creation. In blueberries, beaches, hummingbirds, rainstorms, shooting stars, and growing gardens: "Earth's crammed with heaven, And every common bush afire with God."[1]

And yet, if we're honest, it doesn't all always seem so very good. Sometimes the gardens don't grow. There are thorns and pests and tsunamis and predators. There is sickness and injury and hunger. And every day, plants and animals and people are dying. It can feel challenging to find the goodness when you honestly look at all that is going on

---

1. Elizabeth Barrett Browning, "Aurora Leigh," in *The Oxford Book of English Mystical Verse*, ed. D. H. S. Nicholson and A. H. E. Lee (Oxford: The Clarendon Press, 1917), Bartleby.com, www.bartleby.com/236/86.html.

around you. This does not seem like a perfect garden anymore. How did we get from all of that goodness to this world of death?

Into the creation story of gardens and beauty, temptation came, and a lie, and then the first shattering of harmony. Adam and Eve together broke the rule given for their good, and through that, they opened themselves up to a world that is now disordered and dangerous and is no longer whole and harmonious. By setting themselves up as gods, they paved the path of destruction and death.

The results of this first broken trust are far-reaching. The land is no longer in harmony with people but instead resists producing fruit. Bringing life from the earth now requires sweat, battling thorns, and pain. Death and decay began destroying the goodness of this newly created world. Adam and Eve were taken out of their garden home and became wanderers on the now broken earth.

It is still hard to reconcile how one seemingly small choice—the choice to believe a lie, to covet something forbidden, to steal something not given—could usher in so much pain. How could a bite of fruit result in death and grief and loss?

But the thing is, each of us daily replays the choices made by Adam and Eve. Of course, none of us thinks we would choose death. But we always think we should choose to be in charge. We make ourselves into gods and cyclically repeat the pattern started in that garden. We rebel against the good order established by our Creator, and all of creation follows that resistance. In seeking to become gods, we instead become bearers of destruction.

So what hope do we have for creation? Should we just take the destruction around us as part of the natural course of things? Is there any way for things to be made new?

At the very end of the Bible, there is a picture of the return of the resurrected Jesus. And we hear, "Behold, the dwelling place of God is with man. He will dwell with them, and they will be his people, and God himself will be with them as their God" (Revelation 21:3). And the one seated on the throne says, "Behold, I am making all things new" (v. 5). God has promised that he will, once again, make his dwelling with us. The former things of death and decay and sadness and pain will pass away. Death itself will die. We believe that, in Jesus, God is making everything new.

So where does that newness begin? I'm all for no more tears and pain and no more death and mourning. But how does it start? The story we read in Scripture, which plays out in the world, seems to indicate that it starts with God's work in people. Just as brokenness in the world began with individuals who refused to worship God, transformation comes through people who return to God. Before God changes creation, he changes individual hearts.

The Lamb who will sit on the throne in the heavenly city is the Savior "who loves us and has freed us from our sins by his blood and made us a kingdom, priests to his God and Father" (Revelation 1:5–6). Notice how far our newness stretches: our hideous rebellion—our desire to seize the place of God—has been paid for by God himself who took our place on the cross. He has also made us a community that is learning to listen and trust and give and love. And he has granted us the honor of priesthood—a royal mission.

This call to mission is part of our reorientation to God. It is a shift in purpose, a new way of living. Jesus is restoring us to a right relationship with himself, and through us, he calls still more people. He gives us a mission of restoration that will lead, when he returns, to the whole world made new. This mission is at the center of every Christian's life.

DISCUSSION

1. How have you experienced both beauty and brokenness in the world? How does the world's beauty or its brokenness make you want to be part of Christ's mission?

2. The article mentions the past, present, and future work of Jesus:
   - what he *has done* for you by his death and resurrection
   - what he *is doing* to grow your faith and holiness and to advance his kingdom in the world, and
   - what he *will do* one day to complete his work in you and in the world.

   Why does mission work require such a big vision of Christ's work in the world and in you? Why would a smaller vision not do?

3. Take a few minutes to consider how you would complete the sentences below. Then share and explain your responses with the group.

   One thing Jesus *has done* for me by his death and resurrection that makes me want to join his mission is _____. Why?

   One thing Jesus *is doing* in my life today that makes me want to join his mission is _____. Why?

   One thing Jesus *will do* when he returns that makes me want to join his mission is _____. Why?

PRAYER

Conclude your time praying together for God's Spirit to open your eyes to both the beauty and the brokenness in the world. Pray that he will continue his transformative work in you, and that through this study you will see both your own need and God's abundant grace and power. Pray that the intersection of your need and God's goodness will move you forward in the mission of bringing his kingdom into broken places in the world.

Praise God that, in Jesus, he is making everything new and that one day there will be no more tears and no more death.

ON YOUR OWN

If you would like to study more, read the following essay and reflect on the questions at the end.

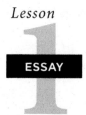

Lesson

ESSAY

Beginnings in Bundibugyo

Twenty-three years old, I stood wide-eyed at the foot of the Rwenzori Mountains in Bundibugyo, Uganda, celebrating Christmas far from home.

Having landed in Africa for the first time only a few weeks earlier, I still felt as new as could be and everything—sights, smells, sounds—seemed utterly foreign. I kept seeking something familiar to land on. But the wildness of rain forest greenery, the sweetness of sun-ripened mangoes, and the rhythms of drumming and dancing surprised my senses with their newness.

Life where I grew up in the Northern Hemisphere means Christmastime is often literally dark because it falls just a few days after the winter solstice, the darkest night of the year. But when you live at the equator, there is always the same amount of daylight and always the same amount of darkness.

Since electric lines had yet to crisscross Bundibugyo's horizon, there was little to no light pollution, and somehow those twelve hours of daily darkness seemed darker there than any place I'd lived before.

Christmas morning itself was overshadowed by a different kind of darkness. In the midst of a celebratory church service and sweet gifts exchanged with friends and a call home to my parents, I also attended the funeral of a newborn baby.

My friend Ernest was prouder of his firstborn daughter than anyone I'd ever met. And though I didn't know the details, I knew that Ernest and his wife had lost other children, but she was pregnant again, and he was over the moon with happiness. After months of waiting, there was suddenly the excitement of hope and birth and life and the joy of a new baby. And then, just as suddenly, the baby was gone—a victim of sickness and poverty, lacking access to resources.

The juxtaposition of burying a baby in the ground while we remembered the birth of Jesus has stayed with me ever since. In my more honest moments, I've wondered: If Jesus's coming to the world two thousand years ago really changed everything, why are babies still dying? Why is there such disparity in the world? And how could Bundibugyo be filled with such beauty and adventure and joy while also being filled with death and darkness and injustice? What is happening in the world?

I came to Bundibugyo with the naive idea that I could and should help people, thinking that perhaps God needed me to somehow fix what was wrong in Bundibugyo. But what Bundibugyo taught me and continues to teach me is that Bundibugyo didn't need me. God didn't need me. But I needed to witness the work of God in Bundibugyo. And to do that, I needed to be confronted by the brokenness of a world of death and loss. I needed to start by asking hard questions about suffering in the world and about a Christian's role in a world broken by sin. And only by allowing Jesus to transform my assumptions about myself, the world, and ultimately about God could I become someone who actually participates in God's mission in the world.

God's mission *begins* with you. You will have to ask hard questions as God changes you. But be encouraged because God's mission *ends* with a new world. God is inviting you into a life of freedom, grace, and transformation. As you seek to understand a life centered on mission, may you always find yourself rooted and established in the God who, by his Spirit and through his people, is making everything new.

REFLECTION

Reflect on the questions below. Pick one of them, and journal about it.

1. What experience do you have with suffering, and how does suffering make you feel about God? What questions about suffering do you have for God? How does Jesus's promise to dwell with his people, wipe away their tears, and destroy death forever affect your faith?

2. The author had to learn that God didn't need her to fix the world. Do you tend to have the same kind of pride, feeling pressure to fix things and people? Or do you shirk away from problems in the world, failing to move toward others in love? Describe how you might need to repent of one of these attitudes.

3. Can broken, struggling, or naive people make good missionaries? Describe what you think it takes to be a useful worker for Christ's kingdom.

Lesson

2

Identifying

BIG IDEA

To be on mission *for* Jesus you must first know who you are *in* Jesus: a child of your loving Father, equipped by the Holy Spirit.

Because life on mission is a mixture of glorious adventures and mundane rhythms and always includes many failures and frustrations, we must learn that we are not defined by our performance. The Bible urges us to look at Jesus instead, and at his surprising, undeserved, perfect love for us. Since we tend to forget this, we must relearn it every day. It is the gospel of grace, which feeds our souls so we can keep sharing it with others. Only as we truly know who we are in Jesus will we find power to love the world.

BIBLE CONVERSATION

The apostle Paul's life was all about missions, but first he had to deal with his identity. Prior to his encounter with Christ, Paul already had extensive religious credentials and experience. As Jesus transformed his heart and life, he became a key leader in the church whose life was focused on the mission of sharing Christ with others. Have someone read aloud what Paul wrote about this in **Philippians 3:4–12**. Then discuss the following questions.

1. Why do you think Paul uses such strong words to describe the difference between his old identity and his new identity found in Christ? What would be the harm of acknowledging that some of those other achievements might also be a valuable part of who he is? Think of several ways this is dangerous.

2. How does Paul's list of religious accomplishments compare with those of believers today? Are you tempted to see your value in any religious accomplishments? Explain.

Paul didn't put aside just his religious accomplishments, but he also had to disregard his past sins. In 1 Timothy 1:13, he wrote, "Formerly I was a blasphemer, persecutor, and insolent opponent. But I received mercy."

3. Are you more likely to think of yourself arrogantly because of your virtues or gloomily because of your faults? Explain why, or give an example if you can.

4. What can you do to stop defining yourself by either your accomplishments or your faults, but instead press on to make your identity in Jesus your own (as Paul says in Philippians 3:12)?

***

Now take turns reading the following article aloud, and then discuss the questions at the end of the article.

Who Are You Really?

Here are some ways I like to think of myself: world traveler, counselor, teacher, friend, writer, researcher, adventurer. I also have to acknowledge that I am often self-conscious, fearful, ashamed, critical, anxious, unkind, or angry.

But faith says that because of God's work in Jesus, this is how I am most clearly defined: loved, known, rescued, forgiven, pursued, redeemed, called, valued. We are defined primarily by the work of Christ on our behalf.

So much of how we experience the world is connected to what we're longing for and who we hope to be. One privilege of living cross-culturally is that it shakes up all of your assumptions about your identity. I was very articulate until I tried to speak another language. I was a pretty good cook until I had to use a charcoal oven and ingredients from a market that sold grasshoppers, cow brains, and absolutely no Kraft macaroni and cheese. I believed that if you worked hard enough, then things generally got better—until I lived in a place where hard workers' lives didn't really seem to be getting better.

The frustrations of living cross-culturally also forced me to face my sin. I was easy to get along with until I had to work alongside teammates in a stressful place. I cared for others until I had to give myself to people who took advantage of me, lied to me, or misunderstood the intentions of the work I was doing. Death and destruction are not just in the world; these evils are in people who seek to be first, who steal, and who shoot at one another. And ultimately, death and destruction are in me.

I respond with anger and judgment toward the very people I want to serve, which reveals anew my own struggles with sin. As Romans 3:23 says, "All have sinned and fall short of the glory of God." I echo Paul who said, "Christ Jesus came into the world to save sinners—of whom I am the worst" (1 Timothy 1:15, NIV). Life on mission is a reminder that Christ came into the world for me because of my sins, which make me the chief of sinners. Only by maintaining the right perspective on my own sin will I be able to offer the world the hope of Jesus coming to save us from sin.

When the ways I defined myself became dislodged, I had to go back to the roots of what makes me who I am. And there I found a story of God's pursuing love revealed in the person of Jesus. The rest of that line from Romans says that although we fall short of God's glory, we "are justified by his grace as a gift, through the redemption that is in Christ Jesus, whom God put forward as a propitiation by his blood, to be received by faith" (Romans 3:24–25).

It's important for a missionary to have talent and training, but abilities are not identity. What matters is not that I am capable or incapable, having been good or having been evil, but that I have received God's gift and was swept into his family. I have a new home.

A friend and I once had the opportunity to visit a rehabilitation home for children who had been rescued from a guerrilla group that recruited child soldiers in northern Uganda. In some ways, the center seemed like a typical Ugandan boarding school. Kids ran around, kicked soccer balls, and laughed. But at lunch, I was struck by one boy huddled over his plate of food. He refused to make eye contact with others and defensively pulled away to be by himself. When I asked our host about him, I was told that this young man had just come back to the center. He didn't yet feel safe. He didn't realize that with his rescue, everything had changed.

This boy was at home, but he lived like he was still homeless. He was safe and protected, but he lived like he still had to defend himself. He had food and shelter and love, but he lived like he was alone and couldn't trust anyone. It would be a slow and painful process for him to come to live out of the freedom that was actually already his, because for so long what was now true had seemed like an impossibility.

Most child soldiers have had to be physically rescued by government soldiers who were fighting against them and were technically their enemies. But the government soldiers went after them to bring them home. Child soldiers are complex because they are both victims and perpetrators of violence. They witness atrocities, and they commit atrocities. They are plagued with guilt, shame, fear, and confusion. And yet, at their core, they are children longing for family, stability, laughter, enough food, and a warm bed. What they need is what we all need.

We are all like former child soldiers. We have both suffered and con-tributed to the suffering of others, but "while we were enemies we were reconciled to God by the death of his Son" (Romans 5:10). We have been rescued by the warrior King who is also our older brother, who pursued in the violent wilderness, and who saved us so we can be restored to our true family. Believing this is a slow process. It requires staying close to our brother Jesus, laying aside who we were without him, and returning daily to the truth of who he has made us.

Hear that list again. Let it sink in. In Jesus, you are loved. Known. Rescued. Forgiven. Pursued. Redeemed. Called. Valued.

In the rehabilitation home, each rescued child soldier entered by burning his military uniform and taking on new clothes. It was a picture of how he was new. He was no longer defined by what he wore when he first came home.

DISCUSSION

1. When you think of being fit for mission, what interests, capabilities, struggles, moral goodness, or troublesome sins do you use to define yourself? How does this affect the way you approach mission?

2. What worldly identity are you wearing that you need to "burn" so you will be defined instead by who you are in Jesus? How would that change the way you live out your mission?

3. Listed below are four pieces of the identity you have as a believer in Jesus. Read through them and think about them. Consider which you would like to understand and treasure better. How might doing so help you serve God and others? When you finish, share some of your thoughts with the group.

> • **In Jesus, I am declared not guilty**. I am not anxious about having to perform for God to avoid his wrath or concerned about keeping righteous appearances or accused by feelings of condemnation. I know I am already forgiven and counted righteous in Christ, free to obey God from the heart. "Who is to condemn? Christ Jesus is the one who died—more than that, who was raised—who is at the right hand of God, who indeed is interceding for us" (Romans 8:34).

> • **In Jesus, I am a child of God.** I have his love and know that I will never be alone or forgotten. I have his ear and know that I may ask him for all good things. I have his constant care and know that regardless of what happens to me, I will inherit all he has promised. I have his fatherly

discipline and know that he works all things for my growth and salvation. "To all who did receive him, who believed in his name, he gave the right to become children of God" (John 1:12).

• **In Jesus, I am holy.** I am no longer defined by my sin but am confident of the power of God in me to fight sin and put it to death. God is with me, strengthening me and refining me, so that Jesus is not just a way to be forgiven but a person whose glory I am learning to imitate and starting to share. "And we all, with unveiled face, beholding the glory of the Lord, are being transformed into the same image from one degree of glory to another" (2 Corinthians 3:18).

• **In Jesus, I am destined for eternal glory.** The treasures, honors, comforts, and securities of the world lose their appeal to me. And the losses, shames, troubles, and dangers of the world lose their threatening control over me. I have a home with God that awaits me, and it is far better than this world. "For I consider that the sufferings of this present time are not worth comparing with the glory that is to be revealed to us" (Romans 8:18).

PRAYER

Conclude your time together by praying that God would work in you to grow your confidence in who you are in Jesus. You might wish to pray for each other according to Ephesians 3:18–19, that you "may have strength to comprehend with all the saints what is the breadth and length and height and depth, and to know the love of Christ that surpasses knowledge, that you may be filled with all the fullness of God."

ON YOUR OWN

If you would like to study more on your own, read the following essay and reflect on the questions at the end.

Lesson

ESSAY

Jesus Becomes Like Us

One of the primary truths of Christianity is that God became human. John 1:14 says,

> The Word became flesh and blood,
>   and moved into the neighborhood.
> We saw the glory with our own eyes,
>   the one-of-a-kind glory,
>   like Father, like Son,
> Generous inside and out,
>   true from start to finish. (MSG)

As we reflect on the importance of *what* Jesus is to us, it is also important to remember *who* he became for us. He is the propitiation, the payment for our sin. His life, death, and resurrection cover the cost of our sin and so we have peace with God. But he is also the God who became human like us and through that learned, in intimate and personal ways, the challenges of walking in our broken world. He came to bear our griefs and carry our sorrows (Isaiah 53:4).

I often have thought about the humility of Christ as primarily connected with the crucifixion: the betrayal of his friends, the mocking from the guards, the beating, the bleeding, and the crown of thorns. And all of that is brutal and shocking.

But the humility of the incarnation started in Mary's womb long before Jesus walked the Golgotha road toward the cross and the tomb. The incarnation is about Jesus putting aside the power and glory that was rightfully his and moving into our neighborhood. The paradox that John reveals is that God's glory, his "one-of-a-kind glory," is actually most fully revealed when he became flesh and blood. Once he moved into our neighborhood, his generosity and truth shone like never before.

In some ways this idea of Jesus being God and also man has become so well-known that it is overlooked, at least in the churched American South that shaped my early thinking about the world. As a kid, I participated in Christmas pageants with baby Jesus in the manger, and every year my grandmother baked a "Happy Birthday Jesus" cake with fluffy white icing and a crèche on top. As a child, safe in my suburban house, surrounded by my loving family, and satisfied by sweet slices of cake, it was hard to imagine why it was such a big deal that Jesus came. I mean, in my opinion, the world was a lovely place to be.

But Jesus wasn't born into my twentieth-century sheltered childhood in the United States. He was born into a small people group who were living under Roman oppression. His mother was not married when she became pregnant. When he was a child, he fled with his family to Egypt as a refugee, and when he returned to Israel, he lived in the obscure town of Nazareth as a precaution. He was threatened, displaced, disliked, and misunderstood.

What I love about these small details of the incarnation is that Jesus, in all ways, became like us. Even in the womb, even in childhood, he did not keep himself from suffering what his people suffered.

And the story doesn't stop there. As Jesus moved through life, he experienced loss, rejection, and sadness—and not because he was a masochist or a glutton for punishment. He did it because he loves the world and particularly because he loves people. And love compelled him to walk with those who suffer, because he "in every respect has been tempted as we are, yet without sin" (Hebrews 4:15).

The definition of empathy is "the ability to understand and share the feelings of another."[1] It is one of the things that makes us human and is the first step toward compassion, connection, and helping others. And Jesus demonstrated full empathy by actually becoming one of us.

Hebrews 12:2 says we should be "looking to Jesus, the founder and perfecter of our faith, who for the joy that was set before him endured the cross, despising the shame, and is seated at the right hand of the throne of God." Jesus knew suffering and death were not the end of the story but that the resurrection would bring rest and joy. He offered himself, like the snake lifted up in the wilderness, to bring life and salvation to all who would look to him.

Hebrews 4:14–16 says,

> Now that we know what we have—Jesus, this great High Priest with ready access to God—let's not let it slip through our fingers. We don't have a priest who is out of touch with our reality. He's been through weakness and testing, experienced it all—all but the sin. So let's walk right up to him and get what he is so ready to give. Take the mercy, accept the help. (MSG)

This knowledge that Jesus bore your griefs and carried your sorrows helps you live a mission-centered life in three ways: by meeting you in your need, by intervening in the world's needy places, and by equipping you to step out into the needs of the world.

First, it means that Jesus meets you today wherever you are. Perhaps you come with shame or sorrow over things you've done or things

---

1. Oxford Living Dictionaries, s.v. "empathy," accessed February 1, 2019 https://en.oxforddiction aries.com/definition/empathy.

done to you. Perhaps you come with fear or anxiety about the possibility of stepping out into the overwhelming needs of a broken world. Perhaps you come with apathy and uncertainty about your role in God's mission in the world. Perhaps you come with anger about the needs of the world or anger toward those who seem to expect you to address needs in the world. Jesus, who loves you, comes with grace to meet you today, just as you are. He is not shocked by the place where you find yourself, and he meets you there with compassionate grace. He fully understands you and is sufficient for you.

Second, Jesus is already meeting the brokenness of the world. Jesus has walked through the suffering and evil in the world, and he has defeated the powers of death with the power of resurrection. As you see the needs of the world, know that his compassionate kindness is infinite. On mission, you move into places of suffering and sin where Jesus is already at work by the power of the Spirit.

And third, his Spirit at work in you empowers you to be a part of change in a broken world. On your own you are not wise enough, good enough, or free enough to meet the needs of the word. But Jesus knows all about your weaknesses, and sends you out in *his* power, *his* sufficiency, and *his* love.

REFLECTION

Reflect on the questions below. Pick one of them, and journal about it.

1. Paul's life was radically impacted by his encounter with Jesus on the road to Damascus, and that encounter allowed him to be radically honest about his own sinfulness and his constant reliance on God's grace (review 1 Timothy 1:12–17). What aspect of God's grace to you do you need to better appreciate, rather than wallowing in shame over failures and sin? How might your life be different if you were constantly aware of it?

2. John the Baptist said of Jesus, "He must increase, but I must decrease" (John 3:30). In a world of celebrity, selfies, and fame, there seems to be little value in becoming less, and you may struggle with feeling unseen or undervalued. But what are some ways God is inviting you to decrease so that he may be greater?

3. What are some specific steps you could take to be like the child soldiers who burned their old uniforms when entering their new home? What does it look like to take off your old sense of identity so that you can put on the identity you have in Christ?

Lesson

3

Changing

BIG IDEA

Through our faith in the gospel, Jesus transforms us in order to transform the world.

Having learned our true identity as children of God, our lives are transformed. We become people who are free to love others because we understand that we are loved, justified, and renewed in Christ. Helping him bring change to the world begins with change in us.

BIBLE CONVERSATION

After taking several mission trips, Paul was arrested and given an opportunity to tell his story before a Roman court and Judean king. Have someone read part of Paul's speech recorded in **Acts 26:9–23**, which he begins by recounting his early days opposing Christ. Then discuss the questions together.

1. How big was the disruption that took place in Paul's life when he met Jesus? Consider changes in his comfort and lifestyle and also changes in his attitude, purpose, desires, and more.

2. How important is it for a person preaching repentance to have gone through repentance themselves? In your experience, what sort of things happen when that isn't the case?

3. Look through the passage and list several things Paul said Jesus does for those who believe. Given Paul's mission, why would it be important for him not just to know these truths as a matter of theology but to have experienced them personally?

4. Verse 20 says Paul preached both in the Jewish region of Judea and to Gentiles, and verse 22 says he spoke to both small and great people. Based on the rest of his talk and what you know of him, what do you think made him able to minister to so many types of people?

* * * *

Not all believers experience a dramatic conversion like Paul's, but all need God's transforming power. Read more about that in the article, switching readers at the paragraph breaks. Then discuss the questions at the end.

A New Home

In between my time in Uganda and my time in South Sudan, I lived for a season in urban America. My neighborhood was made up of row homes, which are houses along a city block that are connected by shared walls. Much of the city was made up of these narrow homes. And in my neighborhood, several of these homes were abandoned.

While I was living in my row home, going to school and living my life, the abandoned house next door began to go through a transformation. For the first year I lived there, it was empty. But then someone came in and started to make the house ready for new life. They began by surveying the situation, sending in scouts and contractors to determine what work would make the place habitable.

The next thing that happened to that home was a clearing out. All of a sudden, there was stuff on the street. Dumpsters were filled with the former internal life of that house—boards and beams and fixtures were hauled away because they had decayed or warped or simply weren't needed anymore. This also meant stirring up all the living things that had burrowed their way into the house under the cover of darkness. Roaches, rats, and other pests had to find new places to hide.

Even though I saw those things hauled away, much of what was happening inside the house was a mystery to me. I could hear hammering and drilling at times, and I could see workmen going in and out. Yet the front of the row house, which looked like every other home on our block, remained the same. Even though great transformation was going on inside the house, creating a space of light and beauty and safety and life, the initial signs were subtle from the outside. Finally, near the end of the renovating, some paint and new windows were added to the outside. But the most important differences happened on the inside.

I believe our lives are a lot like that row home. When we encounter Jesus, he moves into our brokenness, the places in our lives that feel the most uninhabitable. He comes to us, and he sees the parts that feel hidden in darkness. He knows what is broken, what is decaying, what is no longer needed. He sends his Spirit to us to begin the beautiful, internal work of transformation. He makes his home in us.

Initially, that can feel disruptive as things are driven out. The attitudes and desires and habits that have filled our lives get stripped away. The change is deeply internal. What is happening inside is what matters.

But our lives always share walls with others, and so the disruption that impacts us shakes up the lives of those around us. This is a lifelong process for the believer, and God's Spirit is continually disrupting our inner worlds in order to make room for new life and for transformation. This may disrupt the lives who share walls with you. Friends, family, neighbors, and coworkers all encounter the Savior when they see his work in your life.

I've gone back to my old neighborhood a few times since moving back to Africa. And that house that used to be abandoned is now full of life and loveliness. It's hard to remember that not too long ago it was forgotten and abandoned. But we must remember what God has worked in us. In your desire to be a part of his mission to the world, never lose sight of who you were, who you are now, and who you are becoming. Do not forget, first and foremost, that Jesus has come and given you life, transforming your heart into a dwelling place for his Spirit. As you attend to the work of his love, may it spread from you to every neighbor you touch.

DISCUSSION

1. Share something about the condition of your "house." What are some parts of your life God has disrupted or some he is still working on? What difference has it made in the way you live with others who share your space?

2. The article said that when Jesus moves into our lives, he moves into those parts that feel most uninhabitable. How does this make you feel? Why do you think you feel that way about it?

3. Sometimes we are inclined to hide the ugliest parts of our lives, or to try to fix them up on our own to make ourselves presentable to God or others. What does it look like to invite God into our ugly places instead?

4. Consider your life and the difference between basing mission on your abilities and basing it on God's work inside you. How might you fill in some of the statements that follow?

My attitude toward those I serve

When mission is based on my abilities, I _____.

_____

When it's based on God's work in me, I _____.

_____

My time spent with God

When mission is based on my abilities, I _____.

_____

When it's based on God's work in me, I _____.

_____

My interactions with partners/teammates

When mission is based on my abilities, I _____.

_____

When it's based on God's work in me, I _____.

_____

My goal for my mission work

When mission is based on my abilities, I _____.

_____

When it's based on God's work in me, I _____.

_____

ON YOUR OWN

If you want to do some follow-up study on your own, read **John 4:1–42** and the following essay. Then reflect on the questions at the end of the essay.

ESSAY

Believing in Jesus

Life in equatorial Africa, especially in places of low elevation, is extremely hot. When you're there, in the midst of the sweat and stickiness and thirst, it's hard to believe that other climates exist, especially if you've only traveled as far as your bicycle can carry you.

But I know different. I've climbed mountain peaks and failed at skiing. I've spent winter days digging my car out of icy streets. I have frequently interacted with snow and ice and winter. I've tasted and seen snow, and I can't unimagine it.

When I described snow to my friends in South Sudan, they believed it because they knew I didn't generally invent outrageous things and also because they've heard other people talk about it. They've seen pictures in books, and they've used their word for *fog* for snow. Sometimes, I've even scraped ice out of our solar freezer to give people a feeling of the snow. To my Sudanese friends, snow is something that they know is true, and yet they can't quite comprehend it.

Believing the gospel is different from believing in snow. But as hard as it is to believe in snow in the midst of desert heat, it can be even harder, in the here and now, to believe in a world with no more death, goodbyes, and tears.

In John 4, we see Jesus's encounter with the woman at the well. She was someone who knew the ways of the world. She knew she was thirsty and that she had to go to the well every day to draw water. She knew that Jews and Samaritans don't interact with one another. She knew that relationships, even intimate marriage relationships, are fleeting and uncertain. She knew the Messiah will one day come but hadn't come yet.

Then Jesus came and told her everything she'd ever done. And more than that, he invited her into a life she didn't know existed. A life where she would never thirst again. A life where Jews and Samaritans worship together. A life where the Bridegroom is faithful and present. A life where the Messiah has arrived and explained everything.

When the Samaritan woman encountered Jesus, she left her water jar, ran to all her friends, and called them to meet Jesus and discover for themselves that he holds the words of life. So too, when we encounter Jesus, he offers us a world we didn't know existed. He disrupts our assumptions, and reveals that there is more going on than we see or understand. A natural response of a heart transformed by Jesus is to run to those who don't know him and invite them to come to the Messiah.

It can seem foolish to speak about snow in the midst of a desert, and it can seem even more foolish to speak about resurrection in the deadliest of places. How can we talk about faith to people who are hungry, sick, and desperate? Yet perhaps here where it is most unbelievable, it is also most important because those who suffer the most need to know that things will not always be this way. Surprisingly, when you start to talk about the coming kingdom in needy broken places, you will also begin to see that the kingdom of life is already at work in the places you initially thought were filled with only death. Just as Jesus came to the Samaritan woman at the well, so he comes to all of those who bring their hard histories, their empty water jars, and their open hearts.

We may be bringing hope to the next-door neighbor wrestling with depression, to those finding support at the homeless shelter around the corner, to the teen moms at the high school downtown, to the victims of trafficking in Southeast Asia, or to those dealing with post-traumatic stress syndrome in South Sudan. Wherever it is, we all have opportunities to bring the gospel into the most unlikely of places.

Jesus's coming offers us a new way. His life and love offer us patterns of life where all are drawn in and included and there is room for everyone. We see it in the John 4 passage we just read. Jesus drew in the Samaritan woman, and through her the whole community was changed and even the disciples learned and grew. When we personally encounter Jesus and see our lives connected to the lives of the people around us, we can begin to live in a new way, empowered to embrace those who may seem to be the most different or distant from us.

REFLECTION

Read the questions below and reflect on them. Then pick one of them, and journal about it.

1. Do you feel as if you've personally had a disruptive experience like Paul, in which Jesus has cleaned out your old house and made you new? If not, how can you look to God for that? How might it affect your interest in missions?

2. The disciples seem surprised by Jesus's pursuit of the woman at the well. When have you been surprised by the people God is pursuing or by unexpected ways you have seen the gospel spread? How might you need to be more open to God working through people you might be tempted to ignore?

3. When he talked with the Samaritan woman, Jesus was engaging cross-culturally with someone Jews usually avoided. His first move was to ask for help (he wanted water and didn't have a bucket). What might this say about cross-cultural engagement, the role of humility, and how to enter a new place? What do you think it looks like to have a two-way relationship with the people you come to serve?

4. Have you ever felt it's foolish or insensitive to speak about resurrection and hope in a place of death or during hard times? How do we point people to Jesus without minimizing their difficulties and sadness? What hesitations do you have speaking about gospel truths that, like snow in the desert, may seem hard for some people to believe? Why do you hesitate?

4

Praying

BIG IDEA

To participate in God's work in the world, we must be people of prayer and faith who depend daily on our heavenly Father.

When we follow Jesus, we will learn that our own sin and struggles are bigger than we thought and also that the needs of the world are more complex and heartbreaking than we understood before. As we encounter these needs, God invites us to live in ongoing dependence and communion with him through prayer. Prayer is central to a life that receives all we need from our Father, and through it we find fuel and joy for the mission-centered life.

BIBLE CONVERSATION

Have someone read aloud Jesus's teaching on prayer from **Luke 11:1–13**. Then discuss the questions.

1. Notice how the prayer Jesus teaches his disciples begins with two God-centered requests in verse 2. Write these down.

   Request #1: _____

   Request #2: _____

How might your life change if you prayed these two things persistently? What might be different about your outlook on each day? Your activities and actions? Give examples if you can.

2. Notice the three requests for ourselves in verses 3 and 4. Write them down.

   Request #1: _____

   Request #2: _____

   Request #3: _____

   How would your life change if receiving these three things from God were your persistent prayer for yourself? How might your daily outlook, activities, and actions be different? Give examples.

3. At the end of Jesus's parable about persistently praying for good gifts, he says to keep asking specifically for the Holy Spirit. Why is the power and guidance of the Spirit the most important blessing to request? How do you like the idea of a prayer life focused on asking for the Holy Spirit to have his way in you?

4. When serving God is a struggle, you have two choices. You might respond by thinking, *I need to try harder and do better.* Or you might think, *This is totally beyond me. My only hope is to run to God in prayer and let him change me.* What are the differences in the heart attitudes behind those two approaches?

✳✳✳✳

Now read the article together, taking turns at the paragraph breaks, and discuss the questions at the end.

ARTICLE

Daily Bread

No matter what your life looks like today, I bet you and I share at least one thing in common: at some point during most days, we enjoy a meal, often around a table.

What surprised me about life in Uganda, South Sudan, and Kenya is the amount of time given to figuring out food. I've spent days of my life learning what to buy at the market, how to cook with unfamiliar foods, how to navigate propane tanks, charcoal stoves, and high altitudes. I've cooked for teammates, neighbors, friends, students, and strangers. I've made some pretty good meals, and I've had some disasters.

The need for daily bread is one way we are often reminded of our human dependence. Just as the Israelites in the wilderness had to depend on God for his daily provision of manna, we need daily nourishment too. Both the Old and New Testaments explore the idea that our need for daily nourishment is part of a larger dependence on God. We don't live by bread alone but by every word that proceeds from God. We engage with God and depend on his grace through prayer and his Word. When Jesus teaches the disciples to pray, he tells them to ask for "daily bread" (Luke 11:3).

Throughout his life, Jesus himself modeled prayerful dependence on God. The Israelites in the wilderness had not always trusted God's provision: "They spoke against God, saying, 'Can God spread a table in the wilderness?'" (Psalm 78:19). But when Jesus expanded on the manna miracle by feeding more than five thousand people, he offered thanks before the crowd was even fed (see John 6:11). He lived with expectancy that God would provide and with gratitude, even in a world full of needs.

As his ministry grew and expanded, Jesus took quiet time away to commune with God. When his disciples needed to learn how to engage with the Father, Jesus taught them the Lord's Prayer. When he wrestled with his journey to the cross, he spent a night in intense prayer. When he felt abandoned on the cross, he called out using Psalm 22 as a prayer, asking God, "Why have you forsaken me?" (Matthew 27:46). Each stage of his life was characterized by dependent prayer fueled by his intimate knowledge of God through Scripture.

For me, missional work in a cross-cultural setting required more effort and attention to the rhythms of eating and nourishment. I lived in places with no restaurants, no refrigeration, and no electricity. So cooking and eating just looked different, and I realized daily the importance of working to make sure there would be enough food. Though initially challenging and disheartening, I came to love the process of learning new ways to find daily bread.

There are also many ways that work in development and missions can make your normal patterns of spiritual nourishment less accessible. You may not have access to regular church services in your primary language. You may not have options for small-group Bible studies or discipleship groups. You may be expected to have spiritual leadership or expertise. At the same time, you will also experience spiritual battles as you seek to share the truth of Jesus in new places. It can be disruptive to have come somewhere to share your faith and then find your own spiritual life feeling dry.

Just like I needed to prioritize new and more purposeful ways of finding food in Sudan and Bundibugyo, so we need to prioritize new and more purposeful ways of cultivating spiritual dependence on God through prayer. This is the only way to walk through the many different seasons of a missional life with grace and joy.

But even as Jesus offered fish and bread to the five thousand, he also showed that we need something more. While prayer and God's Word are sustaining, they themselves are not the true bread we need. They connect us to the source, but they cannot produce life in and of themselves. Jesus became for us the Bread of Life. He offered up his life so that we could find our life in him. Christ's body broken for us is the source of our life. "For the bread of God is he who comes down from heaven and gives life to the world" (John 6:33).

Though the ways we access and prepare food may look different, all people need daily nourishment for health and thriving. It is the same with the Bread of Life: we need him wherever we go, and prayer and Scripture are conduits that connect us to him. Every day, God prepares for us a table in the wilderness. He brings manna for our daily neediness. Prayer provides a way for us to commune with God, and through that, we can offer life and hope to a hungry and dying world.

DISCUSSION

1. If prayer is so vital to our life with God and our ability to serve him, why do we struggle to pray?

2. The article mentions how Jesus lived with gratitude for what God had provided and with expectation that God would provide even more. Describe the levels of gratitude and expectation in your own prayers. How do they affect your desire to pray?

3. Consider some gospel truths you've read in this lesson:
   - Jesus gave his body to be broken for you when he died on the cross.
   - God forgives your sins.
   - You are a dearly loved child who calls God your Father.
   - Your heavenly Father will give good gifts to his children.
   - You have access to God himself, the source of eternal life, through the Scripture and prayer.
   - Your Father's kingdom is coming.

   Which of these encourages you to pray, and why?

4. Consider which of your needs you regularly ask God to meet and which you try to meet on your own. Then discuss the questions below.

   Daily, physical needs like food and shelter

   ____ I regularly ask God to provide.

   ____ I mostly rely on myself.

   Success in missional work and Christian ministry

   ____ I regularly ask God to provide.

   ____ I mostly rely on myself.

   Exceptional needs such as medical emergencies and family troubles

   ____ I regularly ask God to provide.

   ____ I mostly rely on myself.

   Your commitment to spiritual disciplines such as prayer and Bible reading

   ____ I regularly ask God to provide.

   ____ I mostly rely on myself.

Your growth in faith, godly obedience, and missionary zeal

_____ I regularly ask God to provide.

_____ I mostly rely on myself.

Based on your responses, what things in life do you seek to receive from God, and what do you try to get through your own self-effort? Why is there a difference? What would make you better at depending on God in all parts of your life?

PRAYER

As part of your prayer time today, be sure to ask your Father for some needs you usually neglect to include in your requests. You may even want to pray that God would make you more persistent at prayer or that he would give you more gratitude and expectant faith when you pray. These things, too, are gifts we receive from God.

ON YOUR OWN

To study more, begin by reading **John 6:25–40**, which recounts a conversation Jesus had the day after feeding the five thousand. Then read the following essay and reflect on the questions at the end.

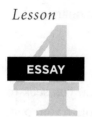

The Bread of Life

Life in less-resourced areas of the world may require newly transplanted residents to work well outside of their natural skill sets. I moved to Mundri, South Sudan, to work in the areas of education and mental health. Before I moved there, I completed a lot of school, read a lot of books, and tried to get as ready as I could. Of course, you can never be fully ready, but I had at least begun to think through what working as a teacher and counselor might look like.

But little did I know, much of my life in Mundri required a whole other set of skills I was not at all prepared for. Things like pest extermination (ahem—rodents, scorpions, snakes, and biting ants: I'm looking at all of you!), cooking with a solar oven, and trying to understand the nuances of cross-cultural humor.

I'm embarrassed to admit that another area I knew next to nothing about was gardening. I do come from a family of gardeners, but prior to Mundri, the only plant I'd kept alive was a tomato plant that grew very tall but never produced a single tomato. Agriculturally, I had not lived a fruitful life.

I also gave little thought to the long-term planning and work it took to get food on the table. I was used to prepackaged grocery store items and convenient fast food. I could grow impatient when it took a few

THE MISSION-CENTERED LIFE

extra minutes for a restaurant to get my food order correct. I had put little time into thinking about the months and years it had taken the components of my dinner to be ready for the plate.

My Sudanese friends were gracious, and they soon included me in all parts of the growing life: preparing seeds, digging in the dirt, dropping in the seeds, weeding the garden, praying for rain, waiting for the harvest, enjoying the produce, preparing the seeds again.

Each step in this cycle felt both insignificant and exhausting. Often it was hard for me, so unacquainted with these rhythms of growth and change, to feel like the work mattered. But when we feasted on greens or peanuts or sorghum bread—meals made from huge plants that I had seen start as tiny seeds—I was able to look back and see the importance of each small part of the process.

Scripture is rich with gardening analogies. For those wondering how to engage with this broken world, perhaps we simply need to be like gardeners: start with what comes next for the season we're in. Perhaps it's a time to clear the ground, or maybe it's time to plants seeds. Maybe it's time to wait for things to come to fruition or to harvest what is ready. Regardless, each step on its own seems small, but by faith we see that the process is producing life and growth and fruit that is greater than we could imagine.

Jesus said,

> Do you not say, "There are yet four months, then comes the harvest"? Look, I tell you, lift up your eyes, and see that the fields are white for harvest. Already the one who reaps is receiving wages and gathering fruit for eternal life, so that sower and reaper may rejoice together. For here the saying holds true, "One sows and another reaps." I sent you to reap that for which you did not labor. Others have labored, and you have entered into their labor. (John 4:35–38)

Lesson 4 Essay: The Bread of Life 49

We understand Jesus's cryptic comment about gathering "fruit for eternal life" includes calling people to faith. But how do we do that?

When people were asking Jesus, "What must we do, to be doing the works of God?" Jesus answered, "This is the work of God, that you believe in him whom he has sent" (John 6:28–29). On the initial hearing, that is the sort of answer I like—believing in God is all the work I have to do! I can believe that Jesus is good and kind and loving.

But Jesus asks us to believe that he is the Bread of Life and that we only live by finding our life in him. This is such a full, whole-life faith that many people who encounter Jesus turn away from him in distress or confusion.

Moreover, many of us who say yes to Jesus may try to work up some level of faith by our own strength. Rather than focusing on Jesus to provide, we fixate on our own ability to trust him. So, we must learn to stop treating faith as something to achieve *for* God and start seeing it as a gift we receive *from* God. Jesus is calling us to a whole life of daily asking, depending, and receiving—for every need both physical and spiritual, even the need for faith itself.

Jesus believes that those who truly receive him because of the Spirit's work will then naturally be a part of others' growth in faith. We will enter into the gardening work that offers life to the world. But the first step—the step we come back to again and again—is believing in him whom God has sent. We struggle to live missionally and to be a part of the growth of God's kingdom because we don't fully know and believe in Jesus. This is why we must always keep our eyes on him.

Each step of the gardening process in Mundri was a challenge. The process was often marked by hope and expectation, challenge and endurance, plenty of waiting, disappointment at times, and in the end, joy and celebration. But we participated in each small part because we knew that all the components, even those that seemed the most frustrating or insignificant, were vital for producing new life.

Our lives this side of heaven are often lived in desert places. We plant and work and wait and wonder what is happening. We want to go out into the world, but sometimes it's hard to just get out of bed. We pour out days or decades of our lives in sacrificial, missional work, and it's hard to see what fruit is coming out of it. But God, who so wisely started us off in a garden, has prepared us for life in this world of seeds and waiting. In the seasons that seem most fallow, things are happening under the surface, even in the soil itself, to bring new life to our world.

Whether or not you ever become a successful gardener, I hope faith is showing you the beauty of all seasons of growth. And I hope grace strengthens you to look toward the future with joyful expectancy, knowing that, from even the smallest planted seeds, abundant life and joy can come.

> And he said, "With what can we compare the kingdom of God, or what parable shall we use for it? It is like a grain of mustard seed, which, when sown on the ground, is the smallest of all the seeds on earth, yet when it is sown it grows up and becomes larger than all the garden plants and puts out large branches, so that the birds of the air can make nests in its shade." (Mark 4:30–32)

REFLECTION

Reflect on the following questions. Pick one of them, and journal about it.

1. The article said, "Jesus is calling us to a whole life of daily asking, depending, and receiving—for every need both

physical and spiritual." How does this kind of life sound to you? What might be its challenges? What might be its joys?

2. How does Jesus's teaching that he is the Bread of Life help you understand him? Along with journaling about the ways in which Jesus is the true bread from heaven, consider pausing at each meal to reflect on how Jesus is the daily sustenance you need most. Or fast from a meal to pray for those who don't have enough food or to reflect on our greater need for the Word of God.

3. When have you experienced the truth that prayer is life-giving? When has prayer felt discouraging or pointless? What helps you pray at those times?

4. Consider how gardening is a picture of missional life. Why do you think God involves different people in different aspects of growing his kingdom? In what ways do you sense God calling you to participate?

5

Seeing

BIG IDEA

Jesus opens our eyes to see the truth about him and understand others.

To begin following Jesus in mission, we first need to see the truth about ourselves, Jesus, and others. Our pride can make us blind, but mission offers continuing opportunities to see things in new ways and to live in the light of God's love.

BIBLE CONVERSATION

In John 8 and 9, Jesus interacts with Jewish leaders who oppose his ministry. It began when Jesus said, "I am the light of the world. Whoever follows me will not walk in darkness, but will have the light of life" (John 8:12). As it turns out, many who think they "see" spiritually are actually blind. Only those who know they have lived in darkness but have received healing from Jesus can truly see.

Have someone read **John 8:31–47** aloud. Then discuss the first question.

1. How are the Jewish leaders blind? Consider what they fail to see about themselves and also what they fail to see about Jesus.

Now pick up the story by reading **John 9:1–34**. You may want to have several readers take turns.

2. What underlying attitudes do the Jewish leaders have as they investigate the healing? List several. How do those attitudes affect the way they treat the man who had been blind?

3. Give an example, if you can, of how a similar attitude might affect the way you treat someone.

Finish the account by reading **John 9:35–41**. Then discuss the rest of the questions.

4. Unlike the Jewish leaders, the blind man responded by worshiping Jesus. How has the compassion of Jesus changed your heart and caused you to "see," so that you have become more worshipful?

5. Why is it difficult for know-it-alls, who think they already see everything about themselves and God, to worship God and to love him and others?

5

ARTICLE

Our Need to See

I should introduce this story by saying that I don't like papayas. Once in a while, when they are sufficiently covered in lime juice and are not too ripe, I'll eat them. But generally, I don't like them.

When I first moved to teach in Uganda, I lived in a simple concrete house where I had a kitchen, a living room, my own room plus a guest room, and a lovely patio and garden. I was learning to navigate the challenges of solar electricity, kerosene refrigerators, and large rats that thought they would be perfect roommates for me. Next door, I had Ugandan neighbors who had large families living in one or two rooms, who had no access to refrigerators or electric lights and were struggling to have enough food.

Every day as I walked down the road to school or bought tomatoes in the market or greeted neighbors, I wrestled with the tension of life in rural Uganda. On the one hand, it felt *hard*. I didn't know how to light the fridge, I hated rats and roaches, and I destroyed the electric system in my house in the first twelve hours I was there. Language study was challenging, and most of the time, at least one person was laughing at me. I thought I was suffering for sure.

Yet I had more than so many around me. I wasn't hungry. I had a mattress, and I had extra rooms no one was sleeping in. If there was fighting in our town, I had connections that allowed me to leave. Sometimes I had chocolate. Each day, I waffled between self-pity and guilt.

Before I moved to Uganda, I held some general beliefs about poverty, development, and my role as a person who wanted to be helpful. I assumed there would be an accompanying sense of peace and calm associated with being helpful in a needy environment. But I was, in so many ways, blind to the realities of life in western Uganda because it was nothing like my life in the eastern United States. As my eyes began to be open to the complexities of life in Uganda, I initially felt disoriented and discouraged.

One typical Saturday morning, I opened the back door to find one of my young neighbors in my backyard. This was surprising because my yard was fenced and the only way he could have gotten in was by squeezing between the bars that made up the fence. In the boy's arms was one perfect green papaya, clearly taken from one of the trees in my backyard. He and I made eye contact, and then he booked it for the gate with his stolen papaya in hand.

This was a kid I saw every day, someone I shared snacks and toys with and generally felt like I knew really well. And he was stealing. From me! I was so mad. I had come to help him and be nice and generous, and he was stealing from me. But here's the thing: I didn't even know there were papayas in that tree. They would have gone bad if he hadn't gotten them. And even if I had managed to get them down, I don't like papayas.

Today we read a story of a man born blind. When Jesus's disciples asked who had sinned to cause the man's blindness, Jesus disrupted their expectations by explaining that sin was not the cause. This shows us that faultfinding is the wrong approach. Looking for what Jesus can do is the right one.

Moreover, we'll grow blind to the mercies of Jesus if we think the arrogant idea that someone else must have been a bigger sinner than we were. We were all born spiritually blind. We all needed Jesus to give us sight, to rescue us from sin, to bring us out of the devil's clutches and into the family of God. That is what turns rebels into worshipers. In this story, only the blind man healed by the grace of God ends up worshiping Jesus.

The grace of God also gives us compassion for other sinners. According to Jesus, the core problem the Jewish leaders had was not their arrogance toward others or their self-serving treatment of the blind man, it was their arrogance toward God. If they had admitted their sin and come to Jesus for saving mercy and had known God's forgiveness, their hearts would have been softer. Instead of judging the blind man, they would have been ready to rejoice over what Jesus had done for him.

When I found my neighbor stealing papayas, my heart had the same tendencies as the Pharisees' hearts. The kid did steal papayas from me, so he was guilty, right? Just like the Pharisees, it didn't even occur to me to ask the larger questions of what was happening in my own heart first. Only later did the Holy Spirit prompt me to ask the kind of questions a person who has received abundant mercy should have asked right away. What cause him to steal? His sinful heart . . . but his heart isn't any different from mine in that regard. I don't steal papayas. But I do steal God's glory and other people's reputations when I judge quickly and speak carelessly. Not only that, I realized his sin wasn't the only sin in the story. What had his family and community taught him? How does the desperation of hunger and poverty impact how you look at life? Maybe I, too, was missing something, like the fact that there could have been cultural misunderstandings at play about whether trees are owned by a particular household or are communal, free to all. But by far, the biggest issue that emerged was my unbalanced selfishness that would allow a papaya to rot because it was "mine" before realizing a hungry kid could eat it, and then to be offended when a neighbor's actions opened my eyes to the ways my selfishness kept another from being well-fed.

Much of development work contains these types of ambiguous situations. What does care look like? And generosity? And accountability? How do people with greater access to resources and wealth work among those with less, while keeping an appropriate view of identity and role? The answers begin with seeing that we too once were blind, and in many ways we still are. We still need Jesus daily. We still need to see our sin, our Savior, and others more clearly.

Cross-cultural work is challenging. It may feel muddy and mucky and really confusing for a while. It may mean opening ourselves up to being hurt or misunderstood. It likely means we will make a lot of mistakes. We can't settle for simple or easy answers; we must continually learn from those around us and from God's Spirit. Thankfully, we have a God whose might is displayed as he brings light to our darkness, and with the blind man we can also begin to say, "One thing I do know, that though I was blind, now I see" (John 9:25).

DISCUSSION

1. Think of a time when you, like the author, discovered you didn't have the understanding and ability to serve God and others that you thought you had. How did you respond to that realization?

2. Consider three kinds of "seeing" in your life:
   - **Seeing your sin.** You consider the full depth of your selfishness and rebellion against God.
   - **Seeing Jesus.** You have deep gratitude and joy for all Jesus has done for you and promises you.
   - **Seeing others.** You notice others, care about their needs, and try to love them.

How do you need to repent (change your self-assessment, attitude, feelings, and desires) to grow in one or more of these areas?

3. How might these three kinds of seeing interact with one another in your life? (For instance, how might seeing your own sin help you be more compassionate toward others? Or how might the difficulties of loving others drive you to see Jesus's love for you more deeply?) Try to give a specific example.

PRAYER

If this lesson made you aware of new ways you need to repent, be sure to include those in your requests to God. Repentance is a good gift he desires to give to his children.

ON YOUR OWN

To study more on your own, read the following essay and reflect on the questions at the end.

Lesson

ESSAY

Seeing God's Work in You

For months, I spent several days a week with Adijah, practicing the rhythms and tones of the Moru language. Adijah was a widow with a rich laugh, a generous heart, and a family to support. I was someone brand new to South Sudan who was bad at language learning, bad at reading cultural cues, and generally a very obvious outsider.

Adijah and I connected as friends early in my time in Sudan, and she agreed to help me learn my new language. As part of my job description, I was tasked with spending several months learning Moru, the language spoken in the small area of South Sudan where I was working. It was hard and slow work, and I felt like a failure most of the time. But I knew that learning the language was important and that it would help in my work of training teachers and serving counselors, so I reluctantly persevered.

On a normal Tuesday, I stopped by her small shop in town, and we sat outside under a mango tree, sipping the tea she generously offered.

I thought I was there to learn the language, but all of a sudden our conversation shifted toward her story. She had shared about her past many times before, but this time it had a different tone. She opened up about the horrors that had happened to her during the war, things

60

common to so many women yet still so grievous and shocking and wrong. I felt such sadness about what had happened to my friend and also gratefulness that she had shared it with me.

She said, "I've never told anyone that before. But I knew I had to tell you because you are my friend. And I want to make sure the same things don't happen to my daughter and granddaughter."

That conversation and my friendship with Adijah were powerful pictures to me of how God works as we step out into the broken world. They showed me that God is always working in ways that are different than our expectations. I didn't really learn any more Moru on that particular day, but the communication we had was infinitely more valuable than what I would have predicted. And my days of language study are what created the space for me to have an unexpected friendship with Adijah and to also gain insight into the work in education and counseling that I hoped to do in South Sudan. If I had only focused on my personal agenda of learning Moru, I could have missed an opportunity to build a relational connection. By allowing God to interrupt my task through a relationship with Adijah, I actually was able to begin the work I hoped to do in Mundri.

Adijah also opened my eyes to a deeper level of struggle and suffering that was going on behind the surface of everyday life in Mundri. I hadn't lived in Sudan during the war, and I didn't understand the heritage and history of violence, grief, and poverty that had shaped my friend's developmental years. But her choice to honor me by sharing her story opened my blind eyes to who she was and enabled me to begin to connect to her in a new and powerful way.

When Jesus healed the man born blind, the disciples wanted to know who sinned so that the man was born blind. They were concerned with cause and effect, guilt and shame. Jesus answered their question by saying the man was blind so that the works of God could be displayed.

He didn't say what the cause was, but he just allowed his presence to bring light and healing into a place of suffering.

Blindness is a helpful allegory for all of us. There are so many ways, even as a Christian, that I remain blind to the work God is doing in the world and in me. I thought I was meeting with Adijah to learn language, but God used the experience to open my eyes to the beautiful work of healing and freedom he was working in Adijah's life.

Jesus came to give sight to the blind and to remove our guilt and shame. We can then both see and be seen. When I moved into mission work, I was blind to the work God wanted to do in and through me. Many of the things I thought were the main things actually turned out to be conduits for something else God intended to do. The people I encountered and the ways we reflected God to one another opened my eyes to see God as bigger and more beautiful than I ever imagined.

I thought I was meeting with Adijah to learn language. But even more, I was there to learn how to communicate hope and love across cultural boundaries. I was also there to witness God's redemptive work in the life of someone who had never been able to share her story before.

When we show up in places of injustice and poverty, we often think we are there to do one thing: teach in a school, work in a hospital, dig a well. And those things are so important. But as we do the work, we also have the expectation that God will continue to surprise us as he does more than we could ask or imagine. He will disrupt our expectations and that is a gift.

Sometimes, we're blind to the work God is actually doing, but thankfully we serve a God who came to give sight to the blind.

REFLECTION

Reflect on the questions below. Pick one of them, and journal about it.

1. Jesus showed such compassion for the blind man: he healed him, shut down gossip about him, gave him a testimony to share, and went back to find him after the man was expelled from the synagogue. How has Jesus met you in similar ways, when you've been needy or when people have excluded you or said unkind things about you? Or how would you like Jesus to meet you in that way?

2. What are some ways God is opening your eyes to new work, either your work for his kingdom or his work in your heart? What surprises has he had for you along these lines? What is still unclear or confusing?

3. How do you most need God to work in your heart to help you see your sin, see Jesus, see others, or see what God wants to do in and through you? Consider writing your journal entry in the form of a prayer that God would help you see.

Lesson

6

Believing

BIG IDEA

Jesus transforms the way we look at the sorrows of this world, including the pain of death.

As we follow Jesus, we will find he doesn't always do what we expect. Death, loss, and suffering will still be a part of our stories and the stories we find in the world. Yet in the midst of this, Jesus brings blessings we did not expect and the power of resurrection.

BIBLE CONVERSATION

Take turns reading **John 11:1–53** aloud. Then discuss the questions below.

1. Describe the disappointment Mary, Martha, and some in the crowd seemed to have with Jesus's timing when he arrived. How is it understandable? Have you had similar disappointments or frustrations with God?

2. Several times in this passage, Jesus said that allowing Lazarus to die and then raising him to life would allow those who saw it to believe in him (the disciples in verse 15, Martha in verse 40, the crowd in verse 42). What makes a resurrection such a powerful sign, so that it causes us to believe in Jesus?

3. Why is it important that we believe in Jesus and we believe he will raise the dead?

4. Jesus doesn't just conquer death in this passage. He also entered into death's sorrow, weeping at the tomb even though he knew Lazarus would rise (v. 35) and setting the stage for his own death to save his people (vv. 50–53). Why is it good that we have a Savior who is familiar with death and is deeply moved and troubled by it?

****

Read aloud the article, "Grief and Glory," taking turns at the paragraph breaks. Then discuss the questions that follow.

Grief and Glory

As the sun rose and temperatures climbed, I drove with Isaac along the rough road to Bari. Early that morning, we had learned that Isaac's twenty-three-year-old granddaughter was at home, having labored all night with a breech baby that would not be born. With each fruitless contraction and passing hour, the mother's hold on life became more tenuous.

South Sudan has one of the highest maternal mortality rates in the world. In a place with poor roads, unreliable transportation, and few options for medical care, this is not surprising. As "the friend with a truck," I had been called so that my vehicle could be the makeshift ambulance to take the mother and child to the hospital. When I arrived, the mom was carried out to the truck to begin what I'm sure must have been the most excruciating two-hour journey of her young life.

Two of my colleagues sat in the back of the truck, giving her fluid through an IV, checking her pulse, and seeking to stabilize her. I drove, trying with little success to avoid potholes and ditches. The strong summer rains had ripped up the dirt roads of South Sudan, and they had yet to recover. But Isaac's granddaughter didn't make a sound. She didn't once cry out in protest to the pain.

We reached the hospital, and the mother was lifted from the back of the truck to a cot and wheeled into a surgical room where her unresponsive baby was delivered and pronounced dead. The mother was taken to a hospital room to grieve and recover.

Tenderly wrapped in cloths, the baby was laid in a box and handed to the family. We left the mother and grandmother in the hospital and headed back to bury the baby. As I hugged the grandmother and prayed for her, she began to sob.

Our journey home was quiet and subdued. As soon as we pulled up to the family home, wailing began around us. I handed the box and baby into the hands of a weeping woman. We gathered around the body, looking into the baby's face, and we prayed and sat and cried and were quiet. In Moru, the women sang about Jesus loving the little children—all the children of the world.

Isaac, the baby's great-grandfather, talked about how good God was to him, and how we had come and saved his granddaughter, and how he was so grateful. I was humbled to see thanksgiving in the midst of such sorrow, and I struggled restlessly to find something in this day to be grateful for.

After many years of work in areas impacted by poverty and violence, I could share many stories about my own personal failures and weaknesses as a missionary. But underneath those stories I can harbor a subtle belief that if I could just "do it right" these hard things would stop happening. Or when I share stories of my mistakes, I can leave a hidden implication that if you avoid the mistakes I've made, things will go well for you in missional work. If you can be open enough, faithful enough, repentant enough, grace-filled enough, then the complexities of missional living will be easier, and then suffering will not be so pervasive.

But that day in Bari, there was nothing else that could have been done. I couldn't change the infrastructure of South Sudan, I couldn't build roads and transform the healthcare system, I couldn't transform the economy so that families could access healthcare. The brokenness that led to the baby's death was bigger than me. I was not, and never will be, anyone's savior. This story is not about me making things better. That baby was, and is, in God's hands.

You've just read the story of Lazarus, a story where Jesus appears to come too late, and Mary and Martha wonder why he allowed their brother to die. How often in missional work have I had the experience of things dying. Hope for life and community and beauty, hope for restoration and change, hope for things made new—these are all good hopes, but they continue to be shaken by the reality of a world of death. Developmental work must always hold the tension of fighting for life in the midst of a dying world.

Jesus himself was a baby chased by death who lived in a time of insufficient medical care and poor transportation options. He had a mother who traveled great distances on difficult roads, suffered much pain without protest, and in the end would lose her child too. Jesus understands, in ways I never will, the grief and sorrow carried by my Sudanese community.

When Jesus arrived in Bethany, he wept and groaned at the grave of Lazarus. He entered into the pain even as he knew the resurrection was about to occur. First the grief, then the glory.

I believe Jesus also stood with us that day in Bari. He grieved for the death and loss experienced in that community. As our living Savior who came forth out of his own grave, he wept with us and gave us himself, and each other, and a kingdom to serve. And I believe his resurrection power is at work. One day we will see him return to claim his throne. One day we will hear him call each of his children up from the grave. One day we will experience all things made new. For now, we grieve. We wait still for him to reveal the fullness of glory.

Lazarus's death and resurrection show us that death is not the end of the story. Here, like Mary and Martha and Jesus, we groan against the powers of the grave. But we know the grave is not the end. Jesus has come and brought resurrection, and so even in our grief we look for the day when the dead will rise and all will be made new. Our work as missional people is to bear witness to the grief and brokenness of the world while at the same time work to display God's resurrection power in new and beautiful ways.

DISCUSSION

1. If you were working in a place where death was all around and seemed to be winning, how might the assurance of resurrection for all who believe in Jesus help you keep going?

2. Why might the promise of resurrection be a reason to start working in a difficult setting in the first place?

3. When Jesus interacted with Mary and Martha, he both offered words of hope and entered into their grief. Which do you do most often when you are with grieving people? How could you become someone who does both well?

4. Describe a time in your life when Jesus met you in your own grief or how you would like him to do so.

PRAYER

As a part of your prayer time together, pray about any godly desires this lesson has stirred: desires to be helpful to grieving people, desires for God to meet you in your own grief, desires to have assurance about the resurrection, or other help your Father can provide.

ON YOUR OWN

To study more, read the following essay and reflect on the questions at the end.

ESSAY

Transformed Expectations

It's the middle of the night, and I'm sleeping under the safety of a mosquito net in a small mud hut. I'm living with a Sudanese family as a part of acclimating to Moru culture. It's exhausting to navigate a new language, new friendships, and the physical work of carrying water and cooking over charcoal. By the time it's dark, I feel ready to sleep for days. Suddenly, I wake up to words you never want to hear in the middle of the night in the wilderness of South Sudan. "Bethany, get up! There's danger!"

Immediately, I imagined all the things you would imagine if you heard those words in South Sudan: soldiers, gunfire, attack. But Elizabeth quickly followed up her statement with the one word that told me all I needed to know about the current situation: "Ants!"

I grew up in the southern United States, and we had fire ants, so I am no stranger to stinging insects. But the ants of East Africa are a whole other thing. They are called *mpali siafu*, safari ants, or army ants. They march in lines, armed with sharp pinchers, and consume everything in their path. If you get in their way, their lines scatter and they cover you, biting and stinging as they go. Their bites are potent enough to draw blood, and if they swarm they are powerful enough to kill a small animal.

When ants take over a house, insecticide is not an option. You just have to get out. My friends and I quickly made our way out of the hut and into the darkness of night. In my blurry-eyed state, I simply followed Elizabeth. She took me over to a neighbor's house and explained to them that I was her guest and that the ants had come. Suddenly there I was, sleeping in the home of strangers who welcomed me in because I was a guest and there were ants and that is what you do.

The next morning, I went back over to Elizabeth's house where I found her bustling around, making chai and getting ready for the day. All the ants were gone. I looked around, and the only evidence the ants had been there were some thin lines in the dirt, showing where they had moved through the night before.

I immediately sought to commiserate with Elizabeth, saying how annoying the ants were and that I was so sorry she'd been driven out of the house the night before. She gave me a puzzled laugh and looked at me, and then said, "But, Bethany, we're glad for the ants. They drive out the more dangerous snakes and scorpions that live in the roof. The disturbance of the ants lasts for a night, but they save us from the greater dangers that could destroy us."

I was struck by Elizabeth's humble understanding that sometimes the difficulties of life are actually working a type of salvation, protecting us from greater dangers. I could only see the annoyance of the ants. But she could see, behind their threat, the gift of protection from things that could destroy her or the ones she loved. Her words had echoes of Psalm 30:5, "Weeping may last through the night, but joy comes with the morning" (NLT).

In the story of Lazarus, death moves into the house of Lazarus and his family and drives Mary and Martha out of themselves and into the saving shelter of Jesus. As Jesus arrives, Martha meets him and says, "Lord, if you had been here, my brother would not have died" (John 11:21). A few moments later, Mary offers the same statement to Jesus. And in their words, I hear echoes of my own questions about missions and calling and work in the difficult places of the world. My heart says often, *Lord, if you were here, my friends wouldn't be displaced refugees, children wouldn't be dying of hunger and treatable diseases, and South Sudan would not be falling back into war.* Especially with long-term work in difficult places, it can become hard to see how God is working in a world with so much death and suffering.

But then, Martha follows her question with this remarkable statement of faith, "But even now I know that whatever you ask from God, God will give you" (v. 22). In the midst of her grief and confusion and anger, she still looks to Jesus. She believes that even after the worst thing has happened, Jesus still offers her the hope she needs.

Life in this broken world continues to confront us with our own weakness. We can't fix problems and can't understand why hard things are happening, and we are prone to fear, doubt, and sin. Death wreaks havoc on the world, and we can't stop death. But we know the one who is driving death out of our houses forever. He has gone ahead of us into death and is working his resurrection power into the world. So, like Mary and Martha, we can continue to step into places of death, loving our brother and asking Jesus to bring his resurrection power into the places we know we are insufficient to change.

Life continues to confront us with stinging ants, with problems and struggles that are real and painful and disruptive. But as we get to know Jesus, we learn to expect what we cannot yet see.

REFLECTION

Think about these questions. Pick one of them, and journal about it.

1. The Bible gives three accounts of Jesus raising a person who was dead (a widow's son in Luke 7:11–17, Jairus's daughter in Luke 8:40–56, and Lazarus), and in two of these Jesus takes his time and at first seems to arrive "too late." What can you learn from Jesus's sense of timing? Where do you need to look beyond what is immediate and believe God's big-picture plan for both this world and the next?

2. During times of disappointment and death in your life, how can you cultivate gratefulness and faith in what you cannot yet see?

3. Why should people who believe the gospel and follow Jesus also be people who grieve?

4. There can be an assumption in missional work that God will protect you in special ways, but the life of Jesus shows that even when you are following God's plan fully, suffering and death will still be with you. How do you trust God's promises to protect and care for you while also acknowledging that the life of faith involves risk?

7

Serving

BIG IDEA

Only by embracing humility, like Jesus, will we find power to joyfully persevere in mission.

As we follow Jesus, we will realize that missional living is more about serving and less about glory. We will find that the journey of faith is marked by humility, service, and repentance. As we live confident in our identity in Christ, we will find the freedom to love others by serving them.

BIBLE CONVERSATION

The evening before Jesus died, he gathered with his disciples. Have someone read **John 13:1–17** aloud. Then discuss the questions.

1. John 13 begins by saying that, in his final hours, Jesus loved his disciples "to the end" (v. 1). What are some other ways to describe how Jesus loves in this passage? How do his actions fit the description "loved them to the end"?

2. Verse 3 says Jesus was aware of his heavenly greatness, "knowing that the Father had given all things into his hands, and that he had come from God and was going back to God." Does this make Jesus's decision to wash his disciples' feet more or less

amazing, and why? How might it explain why he had washed their feet?

3. How might you expect the foot-washing experience and Jesus's instruction to do the same to affect the disciples once Jesus was gone and they became missionaries?

4. How does Jesus's instruction affect you as you think about mission?

****

Now read the article aloud, taking turns at the paragraph breaks. Then discuss the questions that follow.

Lesson

7

ARTICLE

Heroes or Servants?

There seem to be two types of stories about missional work. The first, and perhaps most prevalent, is triumphal. These are stories of work in hard places, of people coming to faith, and of missionaries who seem like superheroes. The second type of missionary stories often come from people who have become disillusioned and see missionaries as foolish or dangerous. Those stories show ways missionaries have failed or done damage. They portray missionaries as the anti-hero. So, is the missionary the hero or the villain? Which story is true?

The problem with both types of stories is that the heart of the gospel, which is the heart of missions, isn't primarily about missionaries at all. It is about Jesus, who came to bring good news to the whole world. He is the one who lived a perfect life, loved the world unto death, and destroyed our enemies through his resurrection. He is always the only Savior in the gospel story.

When I look at the life of Jesus, I marvel at his humility. He came into the world as a baby, dependent on his parents and community. He grew and listened and learned. He made it his work to identify with the rest of humanity.

One of the clearest places I see the humility of Christ is when he washes the disciples' feet on the night he was to be betrayed. Scripture says,

> Jesus, knowing that the Father had given all things into his hands, and that he had come from God and was going back to God, rose from supper. He laid aside his outer garments, and taking a towel, tied it around his waist. Then he poured water into a basin and began to wash the disciples' feet and to wipe them with the towel that was wrapped around him. (John 13:3–5)

Here we see Jesus about to walk through the most excruciating day of his life. But he knows where he came from and where he is going. He is so connected to his heavenly Father that he was able to serve the very disciples who would soon abandon him. He was not concerned with establishing a reputation because he knew who he was and still is. He also knew that true greatness meant putting aside his rightful place of honor and picking up a towel. He took a role the disciples found demeaning. He washed their feet—feet that would become dirty again tomorrow.

Mission work often feels like washing feet that will just get dusty and dirty again. Only when we trust the finished work of Jesus and when we know that we are going to be with him and the Father, will we have the power to love and serve others.

People who serve as missionaries have differing experiences. Many come hopeful and energized but leave demoralized, discouraged, and sometimes even questioning the work of the church in the world. Others work for a lifetime with hope and grace and joy. They work through challenging seasons and experience discouragement and disappointment, yet they seem able to maintain a quiet confidence that God is working even in the midst of failures, loss, and transition. How do they maintain peace and joy when their work feels like failure?

When I first moved to Uganda, I thought I was going to help people. But when I landed, I realized that I didn't initially have much to offer. I didn't know anything about living in the place where I landed. I needed other people to help me shop in the market, cook in my kitchen, and understand the local language. The tables were turned on my expectations of being helpful almost immediately, because I became the person who needed help.

In the life of faith, we are not defined by success or failure. Our identity is rooted only in Jesus and his steadfast love. This frees us to love those we serve without looking to their response to define us.

Obedience to God does not guarantee an easy life—it carried Jesus to the cross. Obedience also doesn't mean honor or glory. Jesus was often misunderstood, overlooked, and even hated. While he was rescuing the whole world, even his closest friends didn't understand what he was doing and abandoned him. And yet, Christian culture today often sees suffering, failure, and loss as signs that God isn't working and that you should move on to bigger and better things.

How do we live on mission? We continue to find our identity in Jesus, we embrace commonality with those we seek to serve, we admit our own neediness and dependence, and we look for opportunities to wash others' feet. Only then will we find strength and joy in missional living and have a powerful witness. After washing his disciples' feet, Jesus told them, "By this all people will know that you are my disciples, if you have love for one another" (John 13:35).

Splashed across television screens, I have seen the great neediness of Africa: pictures of starving children and dying babies and families ravaged by HIV. Yet, living in Africa, I have seen families and communities working together. I have seen people laughing and entrepreneurs successfully building businesses. Even in suffering and poverty and in humble tasks of service, people are God's image bearers, full of beauty and light.

DISCUSSION

1. In your experience, how well do most Christians display humble love for one another? When have you received such love? What keeps us from being more effective witnesses through our love?

2. Some people see Christian vocations or missionary work as having an air of spiritual superiority. Why do people have that impression? How has it affected your approach to missions?

3. Consider ways of thinking about humble service. In each set of thoughts below, there is a gospel response to a way you might be tempted to think. Read through the thoughts and responses, and then discuss the questions that follow.

   I'm willing to serve, but I need to be respected.
   Gospel response: The dignities and indignities of this world mean little when I remember the honor I already have as a child of my heavenly Father. "The LORD is my light and my salvation; whom shall I fear? The LORD is the stronghold of my life; of whom shall I be afraid?" (Psalm 27:1).

   I need for people to notice me and think highly of me.
   Gospel response: Lowly service is true greatness because it is a way to be like my Savior, Jesus. "Whoever would be great among you must be your servant, and whoever would be first among you must be slave of all. For even the Son of Man came not to be served but to serve, and to give his life as a ransom for many" (Mark 10:43–45).

   Life is short. I need to make the most of it.
   Gospel response: Humble service is not a waste of my life but is preparation for the coming life. "This light momentary affliction is preparing for us an eternal weight of glory beyond all comparison, as we look not to the things that are seen but to the things that are unseen. For the things that are

seen are transient, but the things that are unseen are eternal." (2 Corinthians 4:17–18).

I give up! I can't be humble like Jesus. I know he's disappointed with me.

Gospel response: It is not my work that matters but Jesus's work in me. He has washed and fully forgiven me, and now he strengthens and teaches me. "It is no longer I who live, but Christ who lives in me. And the life I now live in the flesh I live by faith in the Son of God, who loved me and gave himself for me" (Galatians 2:20).

Which ways of thinking are most likely to keep you from humble service? Give an example from your life if you can.

Which gospel responses best encourage you when it's hard to serve humbly? Why do they help?

PRAYER

Spend time together praying for God's Spirit to show you the beauty of humility. Praise God for the ways he has pursued you and still pursues you in love. Confess ways you look for success or a good reputation to reassure you of your standing with God or with others. Ask God to grow in you a new confidence in your identity in Christ and to give you freedom to serve others humbly.

ON YOUR OWN

To study further on your own, read the following essay and reflect on the questions at the end.

Lesson

ESSAY

A Life of Humility

Wouldn't it be nice if, when you move to a new place, you could leave parts of yourself behind? I'm particularly thinking about the judgmental, selfish, or prideful parts. At this point in my life, I have lived in four countries, more than ten cities, and countless homes and apartments. One thing is always true: I take myself with me wherever I go.

We've spoken already about the importance of humility when engaging with new cultures. You have to be receptive to growth and change. You will always be learning from those you come to serve. And though it is challenging to accept your need for humility, it can transform your posture across cultures and communities.

But I've learned that sometimes, even when you know how you should be responding in a culture, you just don't want to. At one point in my work in Sudan, I shared a communal kitchen with teammates. In that kitchen was a small stash of Pringles that had to be imported from Uganda. Sometimes we would have guests or interns, who did not realize how difficult it was to get those snacks. They would eat all of them before I could have any, and I would be furious.

Also, our Sudanese colleagues would sometimes compare me with my American teammates. They would talk about my language acquisition, my cooking skills, my weight, or my friendliness. And no matter

82

how they phrased things, I would fall into jealousy, feeling both anger and a desire to prove myself.

Sometimes in my teacher training or team leading, people I supervised wouldn't do things the way I wanted. I would criticize and judge. I got self-righteous and avoided conversations that could have promoted understanding and change.

Now generally, I don't like to think of myself as a person who gets mad about Pringles. And I don't like to think I'm a person who competes with colleagues and who is jealous and competitive about things like vocabulary words. I especially don't like to think of myself as a person who judges others and avoids conflict. Yet there were ugly parts of my heart displayed for everyone to see.

I might claim it was because I was a new missionary. But sadly, when I moved to South Sudan it had been eight years since I first started mission work. I could also say it was because I didn't have enough wisdom or insight, but I had just completed a master's degree in counseling and had been trained as a spiritual mentor through my mission organization. Could I blame it on the stifling, 115-degree days in South Sudan? Well, the weather didn't help, but the real problem was me.

I was like Paul in Romans 7:22–23: "I delight in the law of God, in my inner being, but I see in my members another law waging war against the law of my mind and making me captive to the law of sin that dwells in my members." I wanted to be loving and kind, yet my selfish desires continued to battle against who I truly was and am in Christ.

Paul went on to say, "But if Christ is in you, although the body is dead because of sin, the Spirit is life because of righteousness. If the Spirit of him who raised Jesus from the dead dwells in you, he who raised Christ Jesus from the dead will also give life to your mortal bodies through his Spirit who dwells in you" (Romans 8:10–11). In other words, because Christ is in us, we can live a life of faith, even in our bodies that so often fall into patterns of sin.

This spiritual life begins with repentance. We acknowledge that we have followed our own sinful desires and are in need of rescue. But once rescued, we also continue to live repentantly. We have sorrow over our daily sins. We confess to God and to one another that we have not followed the law of love. We come to see the ugliness of our sin as God does, and we turn away from it, relying always on the Spirit's power. In this pattern of repentance coupled with faith, we can experience a new sense of freedom in the missional life.

As we enter new cultures as learners, we will have opportunities to see our sin in new ways. Cross-cultural living strips you of mechanisms that have allowed you to rationalize or hide sin, so it can seem like you are sinning more when you try to serve God in a new place.

Satan, who is the father of deceit and lies, whispers that you have to hide your temptations and sins. He wants you to think that you must maintain an appearance of success for the people you are serving and the people witnessing your ministry. But we know that the only way to live is to cry with Paul, "Wretched man that I am! Who will deliver me from this body of death? Thanks be to God through Jesus Christ our Lord!" (Romans 7:24–25). Honesty about our continuing battle against sin leads to freedom and hope.

For me, this started with self-awareness. I acknowledged that I was failing to love those around me. Next, I began to ask God to help me see more clearly how I wasn't walking in faith and love. Then I began to confess these struggles to those around me, both Sudanese friends and American colleagues.

Sometimes this talk of repentance can make it sound like you should sit around all day, ruminating on various ways you may have done something wrong. That is not what I'm talking about. Instead,

I mean a relational honesty that is quick to admit to yourself, to God, and to others that you have done wrong, while asking for forgiveness and help. When you can live cross-culturally with this type of honesty and openness, it allows for relationships built on truth, and it lets those who you came to serve see the gospel. In my experience, the times I was able be honest about struggles allowed me to have more freedom and joy in the midst of the difficulties in South Sudan. And they allowed me to be a little less intense when all the Pringles were eaten.

In John 13, we see Jesus humbly washing the disciples' feet. He interacted with Peter, who at first didn't want Jesus to wash his feet. But Jesus said that Peter had to be washed to have a share with Christ. Then Peter wanted Jesus to wash his hands and head, but Jesus said that wasn't necessary because Peter was already clean. So it is with us. We are clean, declared righteous in Christ. Yet when we go out into the muckiness of the world, our feet keep getting dirty and our sinful selves keep betraying us. So the grace of God keeps coming to us, cleansing us while holding out the paradoxical truth that, in Christ, we are already clean.

REFLECTION

Reflect on the questions below. Pick one of them, and journal about it.

1. Where do you feel a false need to hide sins or temptations? Consider both the types of sins you think you must hide and the sort of situations in which you feel pressure to look righteous. If you were more open about your sin in those situations, how might it improve your relationships and service to God?

2. How can you seek the Holy Spirit's enlightenment? Ask the Spirit to show you ways you are currently struggling with sin. Seek freedom to repent honestly and with confidence, believing that in Jesus you are already clean.

3. What are ways you can follow Jesus down the humble path of washing others' feet? Look for specific ways you can love others this week in your family, neighborhood, or church community, particularly if you won't receive any recognition for your service.

4. How do you struggle to live according to the truths mentioned in this lesson? Perhaps you struggle to admit that the battle of sin is a daily part of life. Or maybe you struggle to believe that the Spirit of the resurrected Christ is actually at work in your life, giving you power to repent and live by faith. How you can better live as a person who is "in Christ"?

8

Suffering

BIG IDEA

Missional work flows from an ever-deepening understanding of the power, sufficiency, and beauty of the cross.

The missional life of Jesus led him to the cross. The missional life of Christians keeps them coming back to the cross, finding rescue and hope in the nail-scarred hands of Jesus. The cross is sufficient to cleanse us from every sin and to save us from every effect of sin. By it, we continue to engage with the mysteries of sin and suffering in a broken world.

BIBLE CONVERSATION

Jesus's death on the cross—to pay for our sins and restore us to God—is central to missionary life. For starters, the cross is a missionary's main message to others. Have someone read Paul's account of his preaching in Corinth from **1 Corinthians 2:1–5**. Then discuss the questions below.

1. What worldly wisdom or lofty-sounding messages today might drown out the message that Jesus died for sin? What makes the cross the one message everyone needs to hear?

The cross is also our main message to ourselves. It's where we look for strength to keep going. Have someone read **Hebrews 12:1–3** aloud. Then discuss the following questions.

2. The writer speaks of weights and sins that keep us from running the Christian race with endurance. How do you fix your eyes on Jesus and his death for you? And what sins or weights in your life are you able to set aside when you do so?

First Peter 2:18–25 addresses believers who are in a hard situation: they serve masters who might be cruel. Have someone read the passage aloud. Then discuss the questions about how the cross applies.

3. In tough times, how does it help to know that Jesus suffered too and is our example? Tell about a time this helped you, or describe a situation in which Jesus's example might help.

4. Peter says Jesus is more than an example. He is also our Savior by his death on the cross:
    - He has made us dead to sin and alive to righteousness.
    - He has brought us healing.
    - He has returned us to God.

   Which of these blessings is especially encouraging to you in hard situations? Why?

****

Now read the article together, taking turns at the paragraph breaks, and discuss the questions at the end.

Lesson

ARTICLE

A Mugging

On my thirty-second birthday, I was mugged in Nairobi. Three colleagues and I were headed to an overnight bus that would carry us to a conference on the coast, when four thieves found us. They intimated they had guns and threatened us with harm as they demanded our belongings. Before making off with some of our passports and personal things, one also managed to hit me in the nose, leaving blood streaking down my face and staining my shirt. I cupped my hand under my nose to catch the blood and kept wiping it away in a small attempt to clean up the mess the mugging left behind.

In the midst of such an unsettling event, there was still evidence of grace: a colleague was waiting just across the street, other friends were staying relatively close and came to get us, the bus company allowed us to still travel even though the tickets were stolen, acquaintances opened their home to give the rest of us beds and hot food, our passports were replaced at the embassy relatively speedily, and there was even time for an espresso milkshake from Java House. Though milkshakes can't take away the pain of a mugging, all of that grace surrounded me in the midst of a challenging experience. Despite all that had happened, we reached our retreat only fifteen hours later than planned.

The conference included colleagues working in Uganda, Kenya, Sudan, and Burundi. We spent several days together, praying for one another and reflecting on the rest and joy we find through faith. I had a lovely cottage with a small porch overlooking the Indian Ocean. Every day, a man would wheel his bicycle by, and I'd purchase fresh mangoes and bananas in an attempt to stock up on the fruit that was so often missing from my Sudanese diet. In every way, I was experiencing rest and nourishment after violence and loss.

One day while swimming in the ocean, I looked down to see blood again on my hands. I asked where the blood was coming from, and everyone looked at my nose, which, for no clear reason, had started bleeding again. I cupped my hand to catch the blood, applied pressure, and waited for the bleeding to stop. As much as I wanted to leave the mugging behind me, the wounds took time to heal.

On the last day of the retreat, we took communion. I found my place at the table, tore off a piece of bread, and dunked it into the cup of wine. I remembered Christ's body broken for me and his blood poured out for me. As I brought the bread toward my mouth, I cupped my hand underneath it to catch drops of wine.

My open palm, cupped earlier to catch the blood of my own vulnerability, was now cupped to catch the symbol of his sufficiency. His blood poured out for me—his brokenness my source of healing. It was a reminder that he knows dark roads. He knows being targeted and hit in the face and feeling alone. He brings redemption out of things that seem senseless.

More than that, I saw that I am not just the victim but also the violator. Though I don't mug people and have never physically assaulted someone, my heart isn't so very different from those who robbed me. I steal God's glory so that I look good and feel important, my judgments lash out at others with the force of fists, and I often look out for myself only and don't believe that grace is sufficient. Sin drove the robbers to steal my bag, but sin also drives me to steal for my own glory and hurt those around me if they don't give me what I think I deserve. Though the men who robbed me were guilty and should be held accountable, I am more like the robbers than I want to admit. Seeing my own commonality with the robbers ultimately freed me to begin a process of forgiveness, realizing that all of our hearts need redemption and rescue. When we stop seeing those who sin against us as being fundamentally the same as ourselves, we lose the ability to bring grace into their lives and receive it in our own.

At the cross, Jesus experienced the full impact of sin and brokenness on the world. He purchased redemption by taking the punishment that should have been on me. Only if we fully engage in the story of his suffering, abandonment, and death can we be prepared to celebrate the great joy of resurrection. When I see his suffering, abandonment, and death in my place, I move on to also celebrate the joy of joining in his resurrection.

On the morning before I was mugged, I received a birthday gift of wind chimes created by a company that makes all its products from recycled Kenyan glass. Broken shards, which would have been a pile of uselessness, were tied together with bits of string and became a source of beauty and song. Each time I hear these wind chimes, they remind me of God's work.

My fifteen years of missionary work in East Africa has felt sprinkled with shards. Though much has been great, the work has been harder than I would have predicted, and much of what I've done seems to have been marked by struggle and brokenness. The picture of the wind chimes has been a good reminder that my hope is not to avoid the brokenness. Hurricanes and earthquakes and muggings and good-byes and loneliness and hunger and sadness—all these remind us that the world is not yet as it should be. We look for Jesus to gather up the pieces and shards, tie them together, and create music from what was once shattering.

Our last night in Mombasa, I sat on a porch surrounded by my family of friends. Some kids played cards in the corner. I felt the ocean breeze on my sunburnt skin as the waves lulled us into sleepiness. We sang songs about a kingdom coming and darkness ending and newness appearing. And for a moment, the shards and the cross came together in my mind, and I saw beauty.

DISCUSSION

1. The author was reminded of the cross through a communion service. Describe a memorable time when you were reminded of the cross. What impact did it have?

2. The author mentioned that the cross reminds her that she is both a victim and a violator and that she needs the work of Christ to set her free from both things. Where do you sense Christ needing to set you free from past hurts and wrongs you have experienced? Where do you sense him needing to set you free from the inner dispositions that have caused you to hurt others?

3. Colossians 1:20 says that through Jesus, God was pleased "to reconcile to himself all things, whether on earth or in heaven, making peace through the blood of his cross." What parts of the world feel like "shards" in need of God's peace and restoration? Describe what you hope God will do with those pieces.

4. How might you have a role in God's reconciling work?

PRAYER

Conclude your time together with prayer. Ask God's Spirit to show you the beauty and sufficiency of the cross. Pray for power to forgive those who sin against you. Pray for humility to confess the ways you sin against others. Praise God for his continued faithfulness to his people and his promise to redeem and restore the world.

ON YOUR OWN

To study further on your own, read the following essay and reflect on the questions at the end.

Hope and Cynicism

South Sudan became an independent country in 2011, two years after I moved there. My community was excited and hopeful for the changes freedom would bring. Together, we danced and sang, rejoicing in the possibilities that newness promised. But in recent years, civil war has returned to South Sudan. Once again, friends in my small village are displaced, running from their homes, experiencing loss and instability.

Unable to continue living in South Sudan, I relocated first to Nairobi and then to the United States to take some graduate school classes focused on understanding trauma in international settings. Since returning to the United States, I've noticed in a new way that violence and displacement aren't limited to South Sudan. News from all over the world is filled with stories of escalating disruptions: murderous assaults, racial and religious attacks, politically motivated aggression. It seems violence is found wherever people are found.

As I look at violence in all the places I've lived, I've reflected on divisions connected to tribalism, racism, economic disparity, and unfair treatment. It's clear that whether there's been political independence for five years or 240 years, most of us are anything but free.

So where do we go from here? These are weighty stories that are hard to bear and hard to interpret. It's tempting to make quick judgments or to distance ourselves from reality. We can look for pious answers or the perfect development plan. We can criticize what others are doing, or feel burned out from hearing so much bad news.

During my years working in areas impacted by war and poverty, one of my fears is that I will move from hope to cynicism. It often feels like the obvious jump. Sometimes it seems like simply being realistic. But cynicism is deceitful. It promises that if you are just wise to the world and acknowledge that things aren't getting better, then you won't get hurt because you already knew that things were bad. It allows you to shield yourself from the pain that comes when your hopes for something new are thwarted.

Cynicism also makes you miss so much of the beauty and power of redemptive grace at work in our broken world. Cynicism keeps you from working for change. Cynicism also keeps you from the cross.

Often, I move away from hope because I am moving away from Jesus. I daily forget how much God has done for me through the life, death, and resurrection of Jesus. I stop seeing my own sinfulness and the ways Jesus meets me there with grace and redemption. I am blind to my pride and self-righteousness. I forget about the daily provision of grace I have as a daughter of God, and I miss the hope that comes from living in constant communion with Christ. I also forget Jesus's sufficiency to bear my grief and sorrow. I start to believe that there is not enough grace to change the world because I forget how much God's grace is at work in me.

The antidote to cynicism is returning to the cross. Jesus came for me, not because I earned it, but because of his powerful and redemptive love. Jesus stays with me, not because my behavior compels him, but because his love compels him. As it is with me as an individual, so it is with the world God loves.

When I remember that hope is found in Jesus, my vision for his redemptive work in the world is renewed. As basic as it may seem, when I find myself struggling with cynicism, I go back to Jesus and the cross. I confess ways I have relied too much on myself, and ways I have forgotten my need for Jesus. I remember the ways I have seen and experienced his faithfulness in the past. I reflect on his promises to renew me and to renew the world. I pour out to him the questions and fears that confound me. In him, I find the renewed hope I need.

Much of life today feels like living between Good Friday and Easter, between the cross on the rocky hill and the new life that sprung up in a garden when Jesus walked out of the tomb. But there is one major difference. We now know the end of the Easter story. Jesus's resurrection testifies that one day we will rise with him. As 2 Corinthians 4:16–18 says,

> We do not lose heart. Though our outer self is wasting away, our inner self is being renewed day by day. For this light momentary affliction is preparing for us an eternal weight of glory beyond all comparison, as we look not to the things that are seen but to the things that are unseen. For the things that are seen are transient, but the things that are unseen are eternal.

As we wait for Jesus's return, may we have eyes to see the unseen things. May we have hope in the eternal weight of glory being prepared for us in the midst of affliction. And may we know that in Jesus all the broken and shattered pieces will one day be brought together and made whole.

REFLECTION

Think about the following questions, and journal about one of them.

1. Where do you struggle with being cynical, rather than having hope in God? How can you cultivate hope? What truths about the sufficiency of the cross do you need to believe to address your cynicism?

2. How can you walk alongside others who are struggling and suffering? What does it look like for you to hold out hope to others without minimizing their pain or rushing to give easy answers?

3. We may describe the life of faith as the Saturday between Good Friday and Easter Sunday—we still experience sadness while we wait for all Jesus has promised to do for us and for the world at his second coming. What joys of the age to come are you especially waiting for, and why?

Lesson

Repenting

BIG IDEA

**Because God's fame—not our own reputation—is
our goal, the mission-centered life requires daily
repentance.**

In our hearts, we all resist repentance and would rather keep some of
our sin. But God in his kindness graciously calls us out of sin, not just
at the beginning of the Christian life, but through daily repentance.
Repentance is an inward change that lessens our desire for self-glory
and replaces it with a desire for God's glory, so we can fulfill our calling to love others.

BIBLE CONVERSATION

Psalm 51 is a prayer from David following a particularly evil period
of sin in his life. David's psalm contains key elements of repentance:
awareness and brutal honesty about sin, sorrow and deep regret over
sin, and a desire for godliness that leads in a new direction. Have
someone read **Psalm 51:1–17** aloud. Then discuss the following
questions.

1. What is the mood of this psalm, and what emotions are
   expressed? List several.

2. How can repentance bring out both sad emotions and joyful ones? Have you experienced this when repenting of sin? Explain.

In Joel 2:12–13, God calls for repentance by saying, "Return to me with all your heart, with fasting, with weeping, and with mourning; and rend your hearts and not your garments." This suggests that while repentance may show in outward actions, it is about inward change in the heart.

3. How is Psalm 51, likewise, about the heart? List several ways.

4. Why might saying you're sorry and deciding to change your actions not necessarily be a sign of true repentance like the kind David asked for? What might be missing?

5. Does David repent as a performance for God, or is God actively involved in changing David's heart? Why does it matter? How is David's personal relationship with God connected to his repentance?

✳✳✳✳

Now read the article aloud, taking turns at the paragraph breaks. When you finish, discuss the questions at the end of the article.

Preparing the Way

During his life on earth, Jesus walked different roads through both cities and wilderness and in both crowded and isolated places. He set his sights on the path God laid out, with his final steps taking him up the hill of Golgotha where he was hung on a cross, alone though surrounded by a crowd. His life, death, and resurrection freed us from sin to work for his kingdom. His rocky path to death smoothed our path of life.

But sometimes it feels like the work of missions is more like a disorienting maze than a straight path. We can get things wrong, and sin still has a foothold in us so that the road rarely seems smooth or easy. Isaiah 40:3–5 says,

> In the wilderness prepare the way of the Lord;
> > make straight in the desert a highway for our God.
> Every valley shall be lifted up,
> > and every mountain and hill be made low;
> the uneven ground shall become level,
> > and the rough places a plain.
> And the glory of the Lord shall be revealed,
> > and all flesh shall see it together,
> > for the mouth of the Lord has spoken.

As you may recognize, this is a passage John the Baptist quoted when asked about his mission. In what way was John preparing a highway in the desert? What mountains was he tearing down? Well, he did literally go into the wilderness, but instead of mountains he was seeking hearts brought low as he called those around him to "bear fruit in keeping with repentance" (Matthew 3:8).

Just to get started living a missional life requires repentance. We have to begin by repenting of the ways we've sought to make ourselves saviors instead of looking to Jesus as the source of our salvation. As we do, unmasking the unbelief and false idols we so often cling to, we can then begin to repent of how ambivalence and self-absorption have driven us into ourselves instead of out into the world. As we repent more deeply with God, we are then led to repent more deeply with others. We can begin to repent of the ways that greed and selfishness have kept us from loving our neighbors. We can repent of the ways we have overlooked the needs of the poor and the marginalized. We can repent of the ways some missions have historically used the name of Jesus to promote political or colonial agendas, seeking instead to love others according to biblical standards.

Then, once we're on mission, difficulties and disappointments will stress our relationships with God, teammates, family members, and the people we've come to serve. Sin will arise. Repentance must become a normal way to relate to God and to others every day.

But repentance on its own isn't enough. And repentance isn't an effort we undertake on our own, relying on willpower. The day after John quoted Isaiah, Jesus came to him in the wilderness and John said, "Behold, the Lamb of God, who takes away the sin of the world!" (John 1:29). To make repentance a lifestyle, we must always be looking to the salvation we've received from Jesus, asking for his power to work in us. In this book's lessons about missional living, we have spent a lot time looking at the life, death, and resurrection of Jesus.

This is because the mission we seek to live out is *his* mission. We understand it only as we understand him, and we are only able to live it as we receive grace from him. Repentance is part of that grace.

On the evening he rose from the dead, Jesus appeared to his disciples in the upper room. He showed them his wounds, a testimony that he is the resurrected Lamb of God. And he sent his followers out to offer to others the forgiveness and wholeness he purchased by his death and resurrection. The mission he gave them was about the blossoming of repentance everywhere: "that repentance for the forgiveness of sins should be proclaimed in his name to all nations" (Luke 24:47). It included the promise of the Holy Spirit to make it happen: "But stay in the city until you are clothed with power from on high" (v. 49).

John gives a similar account of that evening: "Jesus said to them again, 'Peace be with you. As the Father has sent me, even so I am sending you.' And when he had said this, he breathed on them and said to them, 'Receive the Holy Spirit'" (John 20:21–22). The repentance we preach and the repentance we practice both come through power from above.

The story of Jesus coming to his disciples and sending them out shows how he smooths a way forward for us. He breathes his Holy Spirit into our hearts and lives. He teaches us how to die to ourselves daily and live for him. We learn to die to comfort, acclaim, worldly rewards, self-sufficiency, getting our way, and having ministry fit our personal dreams. Then we become a part of smoothing the path for others, making a way for the Lord in the world's rough and uneven places.

The world is full of places longing for the hope you already have. As you look for ways to care for this broken world, you must allow Jesus to come into your current places of grief, fear, doubt, selfishness, or disobedience, and transform them through his presence and power. As he meets you, he will also continue to send you out into a world that is longing for resurrection hope.

DISCUSSION

1. How would you like God to work repentance in you more regularly and fully so that you can better serve his kingdom? Do you see more repentance as a necessary hardship or a joyful hope, and why do you think you feel that way about it?

2. How might cultivating a closer relationship with God affect your repentance or change your approach to it?

3. Consider this list of obstacles that might get in the way of repentance:

   Minimizing or ignoring your sin. You make a few small changes but avoid looking at the depth of your sin and learning to hate it.

   Trusting your willpower. You resolve to change in order to prove yourself rather than seek renewal from God.

   Talking a good game. You admit your sin, apologize, promise to do better, and say all the right things, but you have little brokenness in your heart.

   Fixing things or feeling sorry. You work to make amends, punish yourself, or beat yourself up over sin's results, and you let that substitute for heart-level change.

   Which of these is an obstacle to repentance in your life? Give an example if you can.

4. The article reminded you to look at Jesus: he forgives your sin, shares his Father with you, gives you the Holy Spirit, and promises you life with him forever. Which of these blessings encourages you to repent or comforts you when progress is slow? Explain.

PRAYER

Since repentance is an inward change that comes from God, be sure to pray for repentance like David did—beginning now.

- Pray for a broken heart that hates sinful desires, not just their consequences.
- Pray that God would not let you be complacent about sin but would make you eager for change.
- Pray that your Father would help you enjoy fellowship with him and that this closeness would lead to greater repentance.
- Pray that you would repent of self-reliance in fighting sin and that you'd learn to seek God's power daily.
- Pray that your life of repentance would also bring a life of new confidence and joy (the theme of the next lesson).

ON YOUR OWN

If you would like to study more, read **John 20** and then read the following essay and reflect on the questions at the end.

Life in the Garden

During my time living on the edge of the Great Rift Valley in Kenya, I was surrounded by mountains, flowers, wildlife, and so, so many trees. Having moved directly from desert-like South Sudan, the abundance of greenery was breathtaking. Yet in Kenya the vegetation was under threat. Overpopulation and the need for affordable fuel options meant too many trees were being cut down. This led to erosion, landslides, and unhealthy soil, among other problems. So there is a group of guards who both plant trees and monitor the forest to keep thieves from cutting down trees for firewood or charcoal.

Also during my time in Kenya, a group of friends from South Sudan came as refugees to study at Moffat Bible College in Kijabe. When they first arrived, they remarked on all the trees and how beautiful they were. I explained about the work to take care of the forest, and one of them wondered why that wasn't happening in South Sudan. Another laughed, shrugged his shoulders, and said, "That cannot happen in South Sudan. If our nation doesn't care about cutting down people, why would it care about cutting down trees?"

It was a jarring statement that has stayed with me. How do we live and work in a world where people are cut down as though they are of less value than trees? Where the land is destroyed and not taken care of?

Where political structures seem corrupt and self-serving? It can all feel like too much, and the most natural response can be shrugging your shoulders and saying that things cannot be any different.

The only thing that allows us to hold onto hope is the power of the resurrection. At the start of John 20, Mary Magdalene thought Jesus was still dead and buried in a tomb. Death appeared to have won. What did his followers do with their disappointment and grief after seeing Jesus lifted up on the cross?

On the third day, Peter and the other disciple ran to the tomb and found it unlocked and empty. Then Mary Magdalene came back to the tomb, weeping, wondering what had happened to Jesus. She first found angels in the empty tomb, and then Jesus himself appeared to her and called her by name. Later, the disciples gathered in a locked room, afraid of what would happen to them. Jesus himself again appeared and spoke peace into their fear. Next, Jesus came to Thomas and showed his wounds from the cross, and Thomas knew that Jesus is his resurrected Lord and God.

Jesus met his followers as they were wrestling with their grief and fear. He found them when they were standing at the tomb and when they were in locked and hidden rooms. He brought the transformative power of new life into the very places where death seemed to have taken away all of their hope and peace. He knew the grace each of them needed, and he brought it to them.

The followers of Jesus did not avoid the pain and confusion of death simply because they were close to Jesus, attentive to his teachings, and full of faith in what he said. In fact, their trust in him likely increased the pain they experienced through his death. But their closeness to Jesus also prepared them for joy, transformation, and celebration when they realized that even death had not defeated Jesus. His resurrection confirmed that he was the true Lamb of God.

Like Jesus's first disciples, we are not promised an easy life as we follow him into the world. We are not promised that he will work in ways that make sense to us. We are not promised that in this life we will receive easy answers or quick solutions.

Yet Jesus still comes to meet us in the places of our grief, fear, and doubt. He meets us as we stand at tombs, grieving those we love. He meets us as we wander next to gardens and graves, wondering where he's gone. He meets us when we gather with friends, fearful but also finding hope in community. He meets us when we are doubtful and uncertain and need to be reminded that his wounds have accomplished the defeat of death that we all long for.

Every day, there are ways to witness to the resurrection power of Jesus. War can lead to peace, conflict can make a way for restoration, hungry people can be filled, sick people can be healed, sinful people can receive forgiveness and grace, and prideful people can repent and seek Christ's glory instead of their own. But greater even than these tastes of resurrection is the promise that Jesus is coming back. His good work in his people and in the world isn't finished, but one day it will be, and death and dying and sadness will be no more.

I pray today that we will be like the trees of Psalm 1, rooted in the truth of God's redemptive promises, looking for the initial blooming of resurrection hope and reaching to see those promises bear the fruit of eternal life. May we offer life to a desperate and dying world. And may we continue to look to Jesus. He is the master gardener who keeps us rooted in the promises of God. He is the faithful forest guard who protects us from the thief and the fire. And he is the true tree we are grafted into, who has promised that days of eternal fruit are coming soon.

REFLECTION

Reflect on the questions below. Pick one of them, and journal about it.

1. How are you thankful to God for the power of the resurrection? Where are you asking God to move in the world (personal, family, church, local, national, or international) to relieve suffering and bring transformation?

2. Thomas doubted that Jesus was alive until he touched Jesus's scars. In what way is questioning and doubting part of the journey of faith? What doubts do you struggle with, and what helps you in that uncertainty? What in John's account of Jesus's resurrection helps you to believe?

3. When Jesus appeared to the disciples, he declared peace, showed his scars, brought the Holy Spirit, spoke about the power of forgiveness, and sent them out the way the Father had sent him. Which of these actions encourages you as you think about God sending you out, and why?

Lesson

10

Celebrating

BIG IDEA

The mission-centered life is a life of abundance and joy.

Jesus invites us into a resurrection life of celebration and feasting. Despite hardships, we can be filled with joy for what we have today in Jesus and what he promises for the future.

BIBLE CONVERSATION

The prophet Isaiah told of the day to come when God will fully liberate his people from sin and death and fulfill his "plans formed of old, faithful and sure" (Isaiah 25:1). Have someone read aloud the description of this time in **Isaiah 25:6–9**. Then discuss the questions below.

1. Look at the various joys that will be part of the age to come. How might you summarize them in a few main points? Which of them sounds the most joyful to you? Why?

2. What makes a feast an appropriate celebration for people whom God has saved? Think of several reasons.

3. When you think about your hopes for the future or imagine things that might be, how often does this scene from Isaiah fill

your thoughts? What value might there be in thinking about it more often?

Peter, too, wrote about the time to come when we will see Jesus. Have someone read **1 Peter 1:3–9** aloud. Then discuss the final questions.

4. Verse 8 says, "Though you do not now see him, you believe in him and rejoice with joy that is inexpressible and filled with glory." How could Peter say we have inexpressible joy *now*, even though we aren't with Jesus yet? What is it about Jesus and the salvation Peter described that makes this possible?

****

Now read aloud the article, "Grace and Celebration," taking turns at the paragraph breaks. Then discuss the questions at the end.

Lesson

ARTICLE

Grace and Celebration

On Sunday mornings in South Sudan, I would bike a few miles up the road to a small, grass-roofed church. And every Sunday, we would follow the liturgy of Scripture and song, prayers and communion, repentance and celebration. I sat on a small wooden bench in the 110-degree heat, learning the Moru language and finding community with my Sudanese family of faith.

One of the more entertaining aspects of my church experience was that we started singing Christmas songs in July. We'd be in the middle of a time of worship, and suddenly we would transition into singing songs about Christmas and the arrival of Jesus. I'd check my calendar and confirm that it was, in fact, July 15. We were about as far away from Christmas as we could get.

One reason for beginning Christmas celebrations early was that it prepared us for a fuller celebration in December. The songs signaled a fund-raising campaign, a way to begin gathering our resources together and invite all to participate in Christmas preparations. We worked to collect enough money to purchase a cow so that, at least at Christmas, every member of our congregation could have a full and rich meal for free. Over weeks and months, people gave bits of money or bags of sugar or packets of tea. If we had waited until October or November to start our celebration, we wouldn't have had enough to fully enjoy Christmas together. But every year, because of these many moments of seemingly ill-timed songs and generosity, we feasted together at Christmas.

When you consider a life on mission, it is easy to become weary. We may feel overwhelmed by the needs of the world, by the ways we can (and often do) get things wrong, or by the complex situations that influence our choices and opportunities. It can also feel confusing to live in the tension of a kingdom that is in some ways here now and in some ways hasn't been realized yet. And it can just be tiring to keep working in a broken and sinful world.

But God's history with his people is full of joy and celebration. He plants a fruit-filled garden for them in Eden. He brings them to a land flowing with milk and honey and sets aside days for feasting. Then when Jesus comes, he fills nets until they're bursting with fish. With five loaves and two fish, he feeds more than five thousand people and has twelve baskets of food left over. He turns water into the best wine at the wedding. And when he leaves, it is to go and prepare mansions. He is not just a Savior who meets needs but the Savior who comes with abundance.

I think my carol-singing Sudanese community had the right idea. They realized we need continual reminders in order to keep going in the long, dry days that lead up to Christmas feasting. We need times of communal joy, opportunities to share the resources we have today, and reminders that an even greater celebration is on its way.

Today Jesus's return may feel far away, so what can you do to prepare for his coming? Perhaps consider more parties. Gather with others to share a meal or a time of thanksgiving and praise. Testify together to the ways God's kingdom is already here. And keep the party going as you move out into God's missional work in the world. Celebrate—as a testimony to God's presence and grace in the world.

Also, continually return to the love of Jesus. When you fail or struggle or sin, return to the love of the one who came for you. The first mission of our lives is to believe the gospel more and more fully. Only as we see that Jesus is sufficient to meet every need we have and every need of the world, will we be free to care for the world. So return to him. In quiet moments of prayer and Scripture reading, in communal worship, and in every aspect of life, Jesus invites you to experience his grace and sufficiency so that your love for him will grow. As you delight in him, he sends you out again into a missional life full of risks and challenges but also full of the promises of his coming kingdom.

Jesus loves you. He knows your struggles, shortcomings, and fears. And he continues to transform you through a relationship of love.

Jesus loves the world. He knows its struggles, shortcomings, and fears. And he continues to transform the world through the people who bear his image and who are learning to live out of his love.

DISCUSSION

1. What place does celebration have in your spiritual life? What do you do to encourage times of feasting and joy in Christ? What else could you be doing?

2. What are some practical ways celebrating could empower the hard work of missions? Or how might the difficulties of missions require frequent, Christ-centered celebrating?

3. What do you treasure about Jesus and his presence with you that makes him worthy of a celebration even if times are hard and you have little else?

4. Lesson 1 mentioned that we have received some blessings from Christ already, we continue to receive other blessings daily, and we will receive still more blessings in the future. Read through

a few blessings the Bible mentions, then discuss the questions at the end.

Blessings you have received already:

> He has delivered us from the domain of darkness and transferred us to the kingdom of his beloved Son, in whom we have redemption, the forgiveness of sins. (Colossians 1:13–14)

> You were washed, you were sanctified, you were justified in the name of the Lord Jesus Christ and by the Spirit of our God. (1 Corinthians 6:11)

> See what kind of love the Father has given to us, that we should be called children of God; and so we are. (1 John 3:1)

Blessings you receive more of daily:

> Your faith is growing abundantly, and the love of every one of you for one another is increasing. (2 Thessalonians 1:3)

> Casting all your anxieties on him, because he cares for you. (1 Peter 5:7)

> Where shall I go from your Spirit?
>   Or where shall I flee from your presence?
> If I ascend to heaven, you are there!
>   If I make my bed in Sheol, you are there!
> If I take the wings of the morning
>   and dwell in the uttermost parts of the sea,
> even there your hand shall lead me,
>   and your right hand shall hold me. (Psalm 139:7–10)

Blessings you will receive in the future:

> Our citizenship is in heaven, and from it we await a Savior, the Lord Jesus Christ, who will transform our lowly body to be like his glorious body. (Philippians 3:20–21)

The dead in Christ will rise first. Then we who are alive, who are left, will be caught up together with them in the clouds to meet the Lord in the air, and so we will always be with the Lord. (1 Thessalonians 4:16–17)

No longer will there be anything accursed, but the throne of God and of the Lamb will be in it, and his servants will worship him. They will see his face, and his name will be on their foreheads. (Revelation 22:3–4)

Blessed are those who are invited to the marriage supper of the Lamb. (Revelation 19:9)

Which of these blessings especially encourages you as you work for Christ's kingdom? Why, and how? Are you encouraged by all three types of blessings, or do you tend to focus mostly on one type? Explain.

PRAYER

Spend some time sharing ways God's Spirit is guiding you to step into the mission-centered life, or share something helpful you've learned from this study. Pray that a fuller relationship with Jesus would empower you to be part of his kingdom expanding in the world. Pray, too, for a deeper grasp of the grace and sufficiency of Christ that offers freedom for us as we follow him.

ON YOUR OWN

If you would like to study more, read **John 21** and then read the following essay. Then reflect on the questions at the end of the essay.

10

ESSAY

Light and the Mission-Centered Life

In my experience, there are actually two kinds of darkness. The first one is quiet and still with sounds of wind and a creaking house. This darkness means that the morning is nowhere in sight and you are awake in the middle of the night. The second darkness initially feels exactly the same—it looks like the middle of the night. But though the darkness seems the same, the sounds are different. The birds and bugs know what I can't yet see: the dawn is coming, and in a matter of minutes, the morning will begin to show itself. Even though everything still looks dark, in reality, a new day has started. The birds outside my window know this is something to sing about, and slowly I start to see things where once nothing was visible.

Scripture describes Jesus like a light—"the sun of righteousness" (Malachi 4:2). His resurrection on the first day of the week is a new day dawning, a new world beginning. In John 20, Mary came to the tomb very early, while it was still dark, and it was there that she encountered Jesus. In John 21, Jesus came to the disciples just as day was breaking, while they were still finishing their nighttime work of fishing.

Jesus's resurrection ushers in a new kingdom, and his life is what illu-minates this kingdom. But I have to confess, things in my life often feel more like darkness than light. Sometimes the pervasive darkness makes me wonder what I've gotten wrong in my understanding about what is happening in the world.

I'm sure the disciples and followers of Jesus had moments like that as they waited for the resurrection. They wondered if they had gotten it all wrong, if they had mistaken the purposes of God, and if redemp-tion and rescue were actually coming.

But then Jesus appeared. He met them in the upper room, and later he met Thomas. Then in John 21, the disciples were out in a boat, fish-ing. Everything had changed, but they were also still living their lives. At the end of a dark night, they were fishing and catching nothing. But a new day dawned, and Jesus appeared. First, he filled the nets until they were bursting. Next, he sat with them for a meal, breaking bread and grilling fish, inviting them to feast with him. Then he met with Peter and offered him restored relationship and renewed calling. Grace upon grace.

The whole way, Jesus was the one accomplishing the work in the disciples. His grace redeemed and rescued. His grace called his fol-lowers. And his grace guided and sustained them as he sent them out. So too, Jesus's grace that began his good work in us continues it to its completion. A life on mission is first and foremost a life dependent on the grace of God.

Even in the darkest moments, there are signs and sounds of the coming dawn. When I hear the faith of a Sudanese friend who is displaced, when I see Ugandan students I taught now working and thriving and building families of their own, when Kenyan students I counseled find new hope and freedom—everywhere I turn I find glimpses of grace announcing the dawning of a new day. But I hear only the sounds if I am listening for them, if I am waiting for the Lord more than watchmen wait for the morning.

The book of John begins with this: "In the beginning was the Word, and the Word was with God, and the Word was God. . . . In him was life, and the life was the light of men. The light shines in the darkness, and the darkness has not overcome it" (vv. 1, 4–5). The book of John ends with Jesus meeting the disciples at the dawning of a new day. As he was at the beginning, Jesus is still the light and life of men, and the darkness has not overcome him. Our missional life empowered by the Spirit of Jesus walks still in the light of his life.

The last verse of John says, "Now there are also many other things that Jesus did. Were every one of them to be written, I suppose that the world itself could not contain the books that would be written" (21:25). Books and stories cannot contain the fullness of the life of Jesus—the world itself cannot contain his abundance. But as we move out on mission with Jesus, we have more and more opportunities to experience the fullness of the life of faith and the beauty of Jesus who is our life and light.

I don't know where your missional life will take you. But I do know the world needs people radically transformed by the love of Jesus. I hope these weeks spent considering the mission-centered life have renewed your love for Jesus and the world he came to save. I hope you have seen in new ways the beauty and neediness of the world, the sufficiency of Christ, the power of the cross, the gift of grace, and the calling to care for the world. Through that, I hope you have a richer vision for living out a resurrection life in the midst of a dying world. As you seek to live a life on mission, may you find that God's love and resurrection power are greater than all you could have hoped or imagined.

As you begin to think about practical ways to explore missional living in the world, here are a few suggestions:

1. Begin surrounding yourself with stories of missional work, both current and historical.

2. Seek to serve your local church congregation and your neighborhood, perhaps in ways you haven't before. Maybe serve in the nursery or volunteer for an outreach to the homeless, youth, elderly, or any other group you might not normally interact with. Maybe visit neighbors on your street you don't know.

3. Begin regular prayer time for missions, and consider doing this with a group of friends.

4. Look for a way to connect with and encourage a missionary living in a context different than your own.

5. Read literature written by people from different backgrounds and cultural perspectives.

6. Look for opportunities (restaurants, festivals, art, or music performances) to engage with other cultures in your city.

7. Look for opportunities for cross-cultural work or service.

8. Always be looking for Jesus's resurrection power at work in the world.

REFLECTION

Reflect on the questions below. Pick one of them, and journal about it.

1. What meaning and fruitfulness has God brought to your current work, ministry, or service to his kingdom? How might this be directing you to your next work? Or are there ways God is calling you to redirect your work for the good of the world?

2. What does it look like to follow Jesus on mission and work hard for him, while still relying on his grace and believing he is the one doing the work?

3. How have you grown in your understanding of the missional life through this study? Consider how you have understood

yourself in new ways, how you've understood Jesus more fully, and how your vision of God's mission in the world has expanded.

mission
propelled by good news

At Serge we believe that mission begins through the gospel of Jesus Christ bringing God's grace into the lives of believers. This good news also sustains and empowers us to cross nations and cultures to bring the gospel of grace to those whom God is calling to himself.

As a cross-denominational, reformed sending agency with more than two hundred missionaries and twenty-five teams in five continents, we are always looking for people who are ready to take the next step in sharing Christ through:

- **Short-term Teams:** One- to two-week trips oriented around serving overseas ministries while equipping the local church for mission

- **Internships:** Eight-week to nine-month opportunities to learn about missions through serving with our overseas ministry teams

- **Apprenticeships:** Intensive twelve- to twenty-four month training and ministry opportunities for those discerning their call to cross-cultural ministry

- **Career:** One- to five-year appointments designed to nurture you for a lifetime of ministry

 Grace at the Fray

Visit us online at: serge.org/mission